Praise for *This Leaves Me Okay*

"Walter Pryor's intimate narrative of his family is a captivating and often chilling reminder of just how little time has passed since the days when our society cruelly relegated Black families to a grinding struggle against second-class citizenship and a heartless obstacle course designed to deny them 'the American dream.'

Using as his guide the wisdoms of a grandmother whose unceasing letters shaped his heart and ignited his ambitions, Pryor has written a moving and elegant reconstruction of the struggles and triumphs of a Black family's journey from the imposed poverty of segregation to the fragile prosperity of today's divided America.

It is a story essential for understanding the lives of millions of African-Americans, the depth of lingering injuries from our past, and most of all, the extraordinary human capacity to endure or overcome almost anything — with love.

In every family, there is that one child who wants nothing more than to invisibly settle in, near the old folks, and listen, and listen—and then remember forever. Those curious children save our most intimate histories and become the oracles carrying collective wisdom from one generation to the next. Walter Pryor is one of those tellers of the story — revealing the magnificence of humanity in the ordinary and flawed lives of us all."

— **Douglas A. Blackmon, Winner of the Pulitzer Prize**

"In his grandmother's letters, Walter Pryor will forever hear his ancestor's voice. These short, priceless, timeless notes, written in beautiful non-standard English, expose the way old Black people once communicated. The joy of these letters is that they are unfiltered and uncorrected. Now, as Walter tells the story of the woman who loved and nurtured him, we, the reader, get to see how so many Black, rural women lived vicariously through the children they raised. This is a song of praise, a celebration of a warrior spirit who meant for her 'boy' to prosper. As Momma C prepared to go to Washington, D.C., to see her baby graduate, I literally cried. I felt her pride, her joy, her belief that God had not let her down. Read this book, and you'll know how Black people survived."

— **Dr. Daniel Black, author, *Isaac's Song, Perfect Peace*; professor of African American Studies**

THIS LEAVES ME OKAY

Race, Legacy, and Letters From My Grandmother

WALTER PRYOR

 Heliotrope Books
New York

Copyright © 2025 Walter Pryor

All rights reserved. No part of this book may be reproduced or transmitted in any form or by any means, electronic or mechanical, including photocopying, recording or by an information storage or retrieval system now known or hereafter invented—except by a reviewer who may quote brief passages in a review to be printed in a magazine or newspaper—without permission in writing from the publisher.

Heliotrope Books LLC
heliotropebooks@gmail.com

ISBN 978-1-956474-58-9 paperback
ISBN 978-1-956474-67-1 hardcover
ISBN 978-1-956474-59-6 eBook

Cover images and interior photographs courtesy of Walter Pryor
Photograph on page 94 courtesy of the Horton family
Cover quilt created by Lucille Eldridge
Designed and typeset by Naomi Rosenblatt with AJ&J Design

*To my loving wife, Juliette, who spoke this into existence long before
I could envision it, and to Adjua and Osei, who buoyed me
when my doubts might have extinguished it.*

*And for all the ancestors, families, and loved ones
who hold us up and propel us forward.*

FOREWORD

What is it that makes a life remarkable? The subject of this story is one of those people whose impact and influence did not change the world, but who did change the worlds of the people she impacted and influenced. There are plenty of stories chronicling the historic, renowned, heroic deeds of women and men who have attained great success, impacted the world through their contributions, achieved notoriety through famous (or infamous) acts, and/or inspired millions by impressive talent, ingenuity, or luck. But what about a story examining one of those everyday people for whom no monuments have been erected, someone about whom there are no footnotes in history.

I met Walter several years before he reached out to me for some advice about a project he was starting. I had interviewed his wife Juliette in relation to a book I was writing and I also visited them both for an article I did on their home for Yankee Magazine. I was immediately intrigued when he described the project he was embarking upon and learned of the trove of handwritten letters from his grandmother that he wanted to incorporate. I shared with him the process I used to write and gladly referred him to Jeff Ourvan to explore whether Walter might join one of Jeff's workshops. I was excited to get periodic updates that he was making progress and that Jeff was pleased with how well Walter was doing. Needless to say, I was thrilled for him when I was presented with his completed manuscript and asked to be one of his first readers. I'm also excited for everyone who will come across his achievement as it is a touching and inspiring work.

The journey that you are about to take represents a dialogue between the lives of a grandmother who was born into poverty in 1915, lived through some of the worst periods in America's history, and succeeded in building a springboard for future generations, and that of her grandson born in 1965 who benefited from and took advantage of the foundation his grandmother built to achieve personal and professional success, but who also struggled with the obstacles attendant to this country's chronic condition regarding race.

There are instances where the narrative propels you forward in time to underscore the resonance between these two seemingly very different lives that occupy different eras but share strikingly similar experiences. Introduced by actual letters handwritten by the grandmother, these "intermissions" provide opportunities for thoughtful reflection on those similarities while also providing personal and sometimes biting commentary.

This is a book about the Deep South — racism, a family's journey, a mother's love and perseverance — and the triumph of the human spirit.

—Tatsha Robertson, co-author, *The Formula: Unlocking the Secret to Raising Highly Successful Children* and editor-in-chief, The Root

ONE

Like many places in rural settings — what folks call "the country" — it's not unusual to see dogs in the fenced yards of houses along the road. Mangy and barely fed, they often look too old or tired to rouse themselves to shoo the flies buzzing around them. More often, though, the canines seem angry and determined to antagonize anyone who passes. However, in many instances, only the few true visitors to the houses know that the menacing barking, the gnarled teeth, and the desperate clawing at the fence are more show than threat. For once those planning to enter the yard actually set foot inside the gate, the dogs often all but deflate and slink off to abandoned resting spots, only occasionally bothering to even sniff the legs of the household's guests.

In Casscoe, Arkansas of 1920, these dogs became the intermittent playmates and companions for Lucille Hatch and her little sister Dessie Mae at the home they shared with their Uncle Jerry, Aunt Beulah, and cousins. With hair that was just this side of matted and clothes only slightly better than threadbare, the girls might have looked in worse shape than the dogs. But like those dogs, they ran wildly along the length of the fence enclosing them when vehicles or people passed by. Where all these people came from was as much a mystery to the girls as was where they could be going.

Life at their Uncle Jerry's was small and insular, extending only as far as Lucille and Dessie Mae could see beyond the yard. The people in wagons and vehicles always kept going, leaving a trail of dust on the gravel road and taking with them the girls' momentary escape from their little world.

"Y'all gon' be living with us now," Uncle Jerry had announced the day they arrived. "This is my house and y'all be fine long as you do what you told and don't show out. If y'all can't behave, y'all gon' find yo'self meeting my strap — or a switch," he offered with a chuckle. "A hard head make fo' a soft behind. Y'all understand?"

Lucille nodded, pulling Dessie Mae a little closer and behind her, answering for both of them. She was four years old and Dessie Mae only two.

"Don't shake yo' head, girl. You say 'Yes, suh' or 'Yes, ma'am' when somebody talkin' to you."

"Yes, suh."

Lucille was a pensive but happy child, the type who didn't seem to know how to be anything else. Perhaps her cheerful disposition was a coping mechanism that prevented her from sucking her thumb or rocking back and forth to calm herself as others in her situation might have done. Or perhaps central to her being, even as a child, was a will to find the good in circumstances, in people, in life.

She took after her parents in both appearance and temperament. She was dark-skinned like her father and had meat on her bones like her mother. Almond eyes, a handsome nose and a broad, ready smile gave her face an open approachable quality. She wasn't necessarily shy when meeting people — no one was ever a stranger for long. Her quiet charm and warm but subtle charisma relaxed others. When she was comfortable, Lucille shared her laugh freely. Unfortunately, her inexplicable faith in people had already been tested repeatedly at her young age.

"I done told you befo', Lucille. Stop giving yo' food to Dessie Mae," fussed her Aunt Beulah, Jerry's wife. "She have her food. You have yours. You gon' make her fat."

"Yes, ma'am. I'm sorry," Lucille replied sheepishly, knowing full well she had been chastised more than once for sharing food with her sister. "But she still be hungry."

"She ain't hungry," Beulah snapped. "She just greedy. Don't make me have to slap you in yo' mouth again."

"Yes, ma'am."

Lucille knew Dessie Mae was hungry because she cried when she didn't get enough to eat, though Lucille also knew better than to contradict her aunt any further. For that matter, she would still be hungry herself sometimes, but she had learned that there was no point in asking for more. Even though Uncle Jerry's and Aunt Beulah's kids seemed to always get their fill, Lucille had come to realize that she and Dessie Mae always got less. Maybe that's how it was supposed to be since her aunt and uncle made it clear that she and her sister were not their children. Threat of beating or not, that didn't mean Lucille would stop doing what she could to help and protect her baby sister. She would just have to be even more careful when she shared her food with Dessie Mae in the future.

Sad as their situation was, the girls might have received even worse treatment but for Lucille's lack of guile toward her aunt and uncle. To be clear, the conditions she lived under were not lamentable because she was poor. Lots of people were poor. Her situation was unfortunate because the life she was being forced to live was crueler than it had to be for no reason other than the people with power over her could make it so.

How Lucille and her sister came to be in this state was simple: Four years after she was born to her parents, Tommy Hatch and Leola Nobles Hatch, and two years into Dessie Mae's life, their mother died. The sisters didn't have the luxury of knowing their mother long enough to have formed a memory of her. The girls were then sent to live with relatives.

Until an undiagnosed illness that was likely cancer ravaged her body, Lucille's mother had been what country folks called "stout." Not fat, but by no means thin. A healthy, solid woman. Leola bore an unadorned, stately demeanor that might have been described as regal or elegant had she come from a more prominent background. Her family had its roots in Alabama and her just-lighter-than brown skin testified to the family's recent link to slavery, one of the motivations for the family to move west to Arkansas. Yet, her marriage to Tommy raised disdain among some in her family who felt she was squandering the benefits of her light skin given his much darker complexion.

It was not Tommy's appearance or imposing physique that attracted Leola to him; he was not much taller than 5' 7." Although he was strong and muscular, his frame was more wiry than brawny. It was his mild-mannered demeanor and his quiet drive that Leola had observed and wanted in her life's mate. She believed those traits bode well for her and the family they would create.

Tommy was a native of Arkansas, but he was among the first generation of his family to be born there. Like Leola's family, his parents had migrated, not from Alabama but from Newbern, North Carolina, where the family had remained following slavery. Six of his eight siblings had been born in North Carolina before the family's exodus. It is not known whether the threat of harm drove them west to Arkansas or the promise of a better life that distanced them from the family's life in slavery. However, moving did take them beyond the potentially resentful reach of their former owner Richard "Big" Hatch. They succeeded in getting away from him physically though not from his name, which they carried to Arkansas and their progeny have carried into the present. Some members of the family chose to stay behind in North Carolina, too afraid to abandon the place they had known even if it was the site of their enslavement. Whatever courage or spirit of adventure or restlessness that moved his parents to leave their home found expression in Tommy's industriousness as a young man.

Because the United States was born as a rural nation, many people like the Nobles and Hatches lived on farms and in small villages and rural areas in the early 1900s even as the population of urban areas was beginning to climb. As Lucille and Dessie Mae navigated their extended family's mistreatment, World War I had been over scarcely two years and the impact of the war had made life difficult for everyone, especially for people living in the rural South — and even more so for Black people. The marked economic growth that came during the decade was slower to reach the rural poor as the agricultural economy would experience a sustained depression. Living conditions were meager. Racial strife was common. The specter of the Ku Klux Klan made Black life anxious and uncertain. Farming as sharecroppers, working in fields and for White families, and laboring in mills or gins represented the few employment opportunities available to people like the Hatches.

For Lucille, this meant that her father pursued a variety of ways to provide for his family. He farmed a small plot of land, hunted and trapped animals, and sold and bartered for provisions. As a result, he was frequently gone from the family homestead and Leola was the primary caretaker of the children.

The year before, Leola knew that she was dying even if she didn't know the name of what was killing her. She and Tommy had agreed that it wasn't practical for him to raise the girls by himself. Leola wanted Tommy's parents to raise the girls after she died. For a short time after Leola passed, they did go to live with his parents. However, through a combination of manipulation and persuasion, Leola's brother, Jerry, convinced Tommy and his parents that the girls should be with him and his family. Although it wasn't what his wife had said she wanted, there didn't appear to be any real reason to protest since Jerry's house had other children there and the girls were still with family.

The disappearance of their mother and the shuffling from one home to another and then another was disorienting for the young sisters. The difference in the way their aunt and uncle treated Lucille and Dessie Mae compared to their own children was even more confusing for the girls. They could see that their clothes looked a little worse than those of their cousins. And their grumbling stomachs confirmed that they didn't get as much to eat as the other children in the house. Even at her young age, Lucille knew that this wasn't how she would treat anyone but she had also surmised that this was just how things worked. It was perhaps self-protection that would prevent her many years later as an adult from being able to recall much from the time that she and Dessie Mae lived with their uncle and his family.

Like many Black families of that era, geography, and station, the house Lucille went to live in was a shotgun house, long and narrow with only a few rooms situated one behind the other from one end of the house to the other such that you could shoot a shotgun through the open front door and the shot could exit through the open back door without hitting a thing. Relatively solid but not necessarily airtight, you could see the chickens — who shared the yard with the dogs — through the floorboards when they ran underneath the house. Even the chickens fared better than the girls since the yard fowl were fed somewhat regularly and, when they weren't, possessed an instinct to fend for themselves.

People assumed that Jerry and his wife wanted Lucille and Dessie Mae to come live with them to give the girls other children to be with. That, however, was not their true motive: taking in the girls proved to be an easier way to provide for their own family. Tommy regularly sent money when he had it, food that he had grown, hunted or bought, fabric for clothes and whatever else he could come by to help support his daughters and make them less of a burden for Jerry's family. But his efforts were mostly in vain since Jerry and Beulah used the provisions Tommy sent for themselves and their children first.

The inequities the girls endured happened in any number of ways. One summer day — as treats and surprises were rare — the excitement was palpable when Jerry came home with a bag of plums from a house down the road. The neighbors had more plums than they could eat or put up and offered some to Jerry knowing he had his own children and had taken in his nieces as well. Jerry announced the gift as he strutted into the yard and all of the children came running to share in the treasure, grabbing several plums each.

When Lucille stepped up to get two plums, one for herself and one for Dessie, Jerry snapped, "Lucille, what you doin'?"

"I was getting a plum for me and Dessie," she replied.

"You didn't ask for no plum," her uncle observed.

"I'm sorry," she responded, on guard to be respectful. Can I get a plum for me and Dessie?"

"*May* I get a plum for me and Dessie Mae? Don't say 'can I,'" Jerry corrected.

"*May* I get a plum for me and Dessie Mae?" she tried the second time.

"You can have one for y'all to share 'cause you didn't ask right the first time," Jerry sneered.

Lucille didn't hear any of the other children ask for a plum but she immediately memorized the instructions so that she didn't make that mistake again. "It was Uncle Jerry's house and those were his plums" she could hear echoing in her head as she had heard in one form or another so many times before and she knew she had to be careful not to vex him. She took a small bite of the plum — it was so sweet and juicy — but let Dessie Mae have the rest.

Jerry and Beulah at least knew to pay enough attention to Lucille and Dessie Mae when Tommy was expected to come see them. Of course, their faces were cleaned and their hair combed a bit better, but only just enough so as not to arouse suspicion. The girls took baths with the same regularity as their cousins — even if it was after the water had grown cold and dirty; they could wash themselves by dipping their wash rags in the water and wiping off standing next to the wash tub if it wasn't one of the occasional instances when an older cousin had felt charitable and offered to help them.

There were no glaring signs of lack of food or other deprivations evident to Tommy but he didn't visit often nor necessarily take the time to study the girls carefully when he did. Perhaps he couldn't look at them without being reminded of the wife he had lost too soon. Or perhaps the social conventions of his time didn't allow him to express the tenderness he otherwise might have felt for the girls. Given both the fact that Tommy was not home much when the girls had lived with him and Leola, and the fact that they were so young that they had no sense of a nuclear family, the visits never amounted to grand reunions with them running into the arms of the father they missed. To boot, Lucille had no sense of what she should or could tell their father about life with their aunt and uncle.

Regrettably for the girls, from the perspective of a widowed Black man, in rural Jim Crow Arkansas, one generation removed from slavery, not prone to outward displays of affection, conditioned to know that life was hard, and grateful that he had family to take care of his children while he hustled to provide for himself and them, Tommy believed — either sincerely or out of necessity — that his daughters were being cared for and lived where they should be.

For a long time, no one paid enough attention to see what was happening, so no one did anything to make life better for Lucille and her sister. Making matters worse, several family members saw Jerry as volatile if not potentially violent. Consequently, the desire to avoid conflict and a lack of fortitude on the part of those who could have helped them meant the girls would spend a year essentially as poorly tended foster children within their extended family.

Fortunately, one day Tommy's sister-in-law, the wife of Leola's and Jerry's younger brother George, saw the girls racing along the fence in their shabby state and told Tommy what she had witnessed. She would never forget the image of the two motherless girls running in the yard with the dogs.

Surprisingly, upon learning of his children's living conditions, Tommy didn't rush to rescue them or avenge their suffering through providing some merited comeuppance to Jerry and Beulah. Instead of immediately confronting Jerry about how his family were treating his daughters and removing them from their care, Tommy waited. He began gathering information about the household's routines and activities. Evidently, he thought it better to avoid a confrontation or any possible violence that could have erupted now that his otherwise mild manner had been piqued. Or perhaps it took him some effort to summon the courage he felt he needed in case there was a fight. After all, Jerry bested him in weight and height so Tommy had to be strategic as it might be difficult for him to triumph if a brawl were to take place. As the girls endured their aunt's and uncle's inattention and mean-spiritedness, Tommy waited. Finally, with George's help, Tommy "stole" his daughters away while Jerry and Beulah had gone out and left the girls in the care of their older cousins.

On the morning that Tommy and George showed up unexpectedly, Lucille and Dessie Mae had no idea that they were being rescued. Lucille found it thrilling to have a surprise visit from her father and to have to rush quickly to gather her and Dessie Mae's few things to join Tommy and George in a wagon! She didn't know where they were going or why. And she couldn't begin to imagine that their lives were about to change drastically. Yet, in her wonder and confusion, it was hard not to be excited about whatever was coming next.

It wasn't quite noon so the sun wasn't at the top of the sky yet, but it was already proving to be a beautiful day. For Lucille and Dessie Mae, the world suddenly felt bigger and greener and brighter just sitting in the wagon, outside the fence. The fields around the house they were about to leave stretched as far as the eye could see in every direction. Rows of rice and soybeans were verdant against rich, dark soil. The blue of the sky seemed to pull them into it. Somehow for the first time, Lucille saw a forest of trees that swallowed the road in the distance.

With her arms tight around her little sister, Lucille rocked back and forth from the slow steady movement of the wagon in the rutted road. Unfortunately, closing this unhappy chapter of torment and neglect would not shield Lucille from even rougher trials and heartache to come. But no matter what lay ahead, if nothing else, things at least were going to be different. Now, like all those people they ran to watch pass, it was their turn to leave behind the ramshackle house with its associated mistreatment and family who had failed them . . . and the dogs whose barking grew fainter and fainter the farther they traveled down the road.

TWO

My grandmother, Lucille Hatch Eldridge, wrote letters to me for nearly the entire time that we shared the planet. Even before I could read, my mother read to my sister and me letters from my grandmother. In fact, I have few memories that come before my remembrance of receiving regular missives from "Mama Ceal" as we called her — among them getting in trouble for peeing outside in the backyard with my friend Clemmie who lived down the street from my Aunt Elizabeth; licking the sugar off the little bells that decorated my parents' wedding cake; and a recurring dream in which I was chased by a bear but that always was interrupted by a voice-over narrator speculating whether I would escape and encouraging "viewers" to "tune in next week" to learn my fate.

Because Mama Ceal's letters came almost weekly, as I got older, I had the luxury of taking them for granted. Yet, every time I received a letter, it felt like an unexpected gift that shook me out of whatever occupied my thinking at the time. Although there was nothing in the letter referencing old memories or some forgotten piece of family lore, for a few moments, I was instantly returned to the warmth and intimacy of a childhood hug. Her letters came to represent a familiar, consistent, sustaining expression of love and concern that connected and grounded and comforted me, regardless of how old I was or where I was in my life.

The letters from my grandmother weren't remarkable in and of themselves. She wasn't one to share deep mysteries or sage, anecdotal mother-wit. I'm not even sure she ever gave me much practical advice in the letters beyond reminding me to remember to pray. Instead, on their face, the letters, like the one that follows, were often simple chronicles of what had transpired since her last writing. They might contain a recipe as this one did or a news clipping that she found interesting. Or she might express her anticipation of an upcoming trip or event. Sometimes the letters shared a bit of news about the family for whom she worked for over 40 years. Or they might just reflect what was most prominent in her mind when she sat down to write. Here is one that I received in September of 1988:

> Route 1 Box 318
> Forrest City Ark
> Dear Grandson
> well this leve me all, thank the Lord hope you are all write and happy you be a good boy I saw mattie and diann at the Craf Shaw in Forrest City she say she were proud of you all because its so meny have days on drugs & dum nather but you is tryeng to make something out of your self. She say keep on. She is proud of you and Jackie and realy proud of you mather for the way She have train you Bam Bam say Hi and they is real proud of you they say bee a good boy and keep praying they is prayeing for you two

And Aunt Rubbie is so Proud of you all Laurence is home But they dont thank it hat fare long becaus Rubbie Cant wait on him She is Sick too here is a Grauma's resip its Grandma's Cookies

½ cup Butter margen 1 cup Sugar 3 eggs dash of salt 1 cup all Purpase Flour ¾ cup Chocolate syrup Canned 2 tsp. Vanilla ¾ cup pecans or nat 1 in a bowl Cream together Butter Sugar gnd add eggs mix until very creamy add salt Sif flour mix well add Chocolate syrup Vanilla Chopped nuts or bur but greased + flour a 9 in. pan Smooth top Bake at 350° about 35 min. Cool on wire rack loose at edge Cut in Squares garnish nuts or Pouder Sugar

Route 1 Box 315
Forrest City, Ark

Dear Grandson,

Well this leve me ok. Thank the Lord. Hope you are all write and happy. You be a good boy. I saw Mattie and Diann at the craf show in Forrest City. She say she were proud of you all because its so many now days on drugs and durin nothen, But you is trying to make something out of yourself. She say keep on. She is proud of you and Jackie. And realy proud of your mother fore the way she have train you. Bam Bam say hi and they is real proud of you. They say bee a good boy and keep praying. They is praying fore you two. And Aunt Rubbie is so proud of you all. Lawrence is home but they dont thank it not for long becaus Rubbie cant wait on him. She is sick two. Here is a brownies resip. Its [from] Grandma's Cookies.

½ cup butter [or] margen 1 cup sugar 3 eggs Dash of salt
1cup All Purpose flour
¾ cup chocolate syrup canned
2 tsp vanilla ¾ cup pecans or nut

In a bowl cream together butter [&] sugar good. Add eggs. Mix until very creamy. Add salt. Sif [sift] flour. Mix well. Add Chocolate syrup, vanilla, chopped nuts or leve out. Greased & flour a 9 in pan. Smooth top. Bake at 350° F [for] about 35 min. Cool on wire rack. Loose at edge. Cut in squares. Garnish [with] nuts or powder sugar.

What is remarkable about her letters is that she sat down to write at all. My grandmother had only an eighth-grade education which she received at a time in our country's history when schooling for Black children — especially those who were living in southern rural areas like Madison, Arkansas — was not well funded. As a result, the quality of education varied widely and was severely lacking in comparison to the education afforded White children. It is not surprising then that Mama Ceal's letters demonstrate that her grammar was fickle and her handwriting sometimes unclear. Those details, however, endear them — and her — to me even more.

The act of letter writing was not common for someone of her station. What would motivate a Black woman who spent most of her life as a maid to devote precious free time writing letters when she could be enjoying one of her crafts or resting and doing nothing at all? Why hadn't conventional thought and wisdom discouraged her from taking up this pastime that was not only unusual for people like her but was prohibited for her forebearers? She wasn't well read or knowledgeable of the great Black writers of the era. She had not been exposed to the letters of famous historical figures. Moreover, it is clear that she did not have a sense of having a place in history and did not see herself as anyone of great import. In this context, the letters take on an even more curious life since she likely had no expectation of them surviving beyond their initial reading. Yet, her thoughts and words as captured in her letters reflect a slice of everyday Black rural Southern Americana.

What also makes the letters remarkable for me is what they came to represent, first as a young child and then as an adult. Admittedly, that the letters evoked such sentimentality in me perhaps speaks less about the letters themselves than what it reveals about me. In the simplest of terms, Mama Ceal's letters were a refuge for a little boy lost in conundrums not all of which were of his making and an anchor for a young man navigating unchartered territory while balancing self-confidence and doubt.

I was four years old in 1969 and by then I had heard a lot that I was an "old" soul. Perhaps they meant I didn't often act like a child and took more of an interest in "grown folks' business" than what they considered children's matters. I do remember thinking to myself as a young kid that I wished grownups realized that I knew a lot more than they thought. I was also a very sensitive soul as well, one who experienced emotion much more acutely than the adults around me noticed or imagined. The intensity of the joy I felt from a spontaneous hug or praise of some accomplishment was matched by the intensity of the hurt I felt from a perceived slight or undeserved chiding. The truth is I lived inside my head a lot.

My parents were not married when my sister and I were born. My father was in the middle of extracting himself from his first marriage when he met my mother, a college student at Arkansas Agricultural, Mechanical and Normal College ("AM&N"), a historically Black college in Pine Bluff, Arkansas with a solid reputation, roughly two hours from my mother's hometown of Forrest City, Arkansas. He, an older, good-looking man who had served in World War II and who could have a larger-than-life personality. She, an attractive young woman who did not appreciate her own beauty and who was a bit self-conscious and reserved. Their romance led to the births of my sister and me before their marriage several years later. Thus, we — my mother, sister, and I — lived with our Aunt Elizabeth, or

"Momo" as we called her, and Uncle Owen ("Papa") for the first five years of my life until after my parents wed and the four of us lived together.

Before then, visits from my father to Momo and Papa's house — our house — were "events" from my vantage point. Although I rarely knew in advance when he was coming to visit, there was a clear air of anticipation if we did happen to overhear that he was coming. I remember thinking he was fun and how I would be caught up in the excitement of him being there. However, he also seemed a bit gruff to me and I wasn't sure if he really liked me in the way that he seemed to adore my sister. Gruff, however, wasn't new or difficult to manage since Momo was a strict disciplinarian who didn't suffer ill-behaved children. Gruff I could do.

I always loved my mother but, as a young child, I lacked clarity of her role in my life. The dynamic in Momo & Papa's house was that Momo was the "parent" and my mother was more like an older sibling. Both my mother and Papa deferred to Momo in how I was raised. It is strange only in my recalling of it, but didn't seem so at the time since it was all I knew. What I do know is that even as an old, sensitive soul, what I could not have articulated was that I craved a nurturing that was not there during those early years. While this dynamic changed somewhat after my parents married and we lived together, the imprint of it was strong for me and created a longing for emotional mooring.

Partly for the entertainment value of it and partly because of the ache for emotional connection, I became a child who loved television. I loved television more than anything: more than riding in my little metal pedal car that I loved "driving" until I was too big to squeeze into it, more than playing with friends, and even more than riding bikes and disappearing for hours at a time as an older adolescent. I loved television so much that it was often the case that I was made to turn off the TV and go find something to do outside.

I didn't realized it at the time but the TV was a means of escape and compensation: escape into a world that was foreign to my daily existence and compensation for the stronger emotional anchoring that I wasn't getting. In the world of television, life seemed easy, where there was no lack; where a mother and father and their children were demonstratively loving; where punishments didn't involve switches a kid had to pick for himself; and where any problem or disagreement was quickly resolved in a matter of 30 minutes or, at most, an hour.

Oddly enough, when I developed my adoration for TV, my life was generally very good. I was not abused or mistreated. I never knew what it was to be hungry or feel destitute —though at times we probably were just barely above poor. One of my fondest memories is how Momo took our sneakers — think Chuck Taylor Converse but the no-name version — and cut the toe cover off the top and cut holes along the sides and at the heels to create makeshift "sandals" to extend the wear and delay having to purchase another pair given how quickly we outgrew them. I had no idea this was a money-saving tactic and thought they were one of the coolest things a kid could have.

I loved the hokey sentimentality of family that I saw on TV. The families on television and in the old black and white movies had a lot of it. They also seemed to have so much more fun. They played games as a family. They went out to eat at restaurants. They went on vacation. They entertained. They went on picnics. They flew on airplanes and traveled on cruise ships. They didn't eat beans and cornbread or food they had grown in their gardens. They didn't paste S&H green stamps in coupon books. Their lives seemed brighter and shinier and richer. And so, despite the fact none of those families were Black or looked like mine, I envied and consumed their lives. It is also possible that it was because none of the TV families were Black that I was so taken with them. Whatever the underlying reason, the escape of TV provided me access to an existence that at the time seemed much better than my own.

It wasn't until I was an adult with children of my own that I learned that my grandmother had compelling reasons to want to escape her childhood as well. I came to appreciate that those experiences impacted her in ways that would reverberate so much that I felt them too.

THREE

In yet another shuffle, Lucille and her little sister went to live with their grandparents, Tommy's mother and father. In this instance, the move was most definitely for the better.

The girls' new home in Almyra, though still in Arkansas County, was approximately 20 miles from the shotgun house they had shared with their Uncle Jerry and his family in Casscoe, which equaled an eight-hour walk, a three-to-four hour wagon ride and an hour or less drive by car. Although the actual distance between their old home and their new one wasn't especially far, it felt like the other side of the world for Lucille.

Tommy's parents, Edward and Liza, were the patriarch and matriarch of the Arkansas branch of the Hatch family. They had marshaled adventurous spirits and blind courage to risk the trek moving their family of five children from North Carolina to Arkansas. Most importantly for the girls, Edward and Liza had kind, compassionate hearts and were especially loving towards their granddaughters. They instinctively recognized — in a way Tommy seemed oblivious to — that the girls needed a real home.

Jerry and Beulah never came to retrieve the girls and there was no reason for them to do so since Tommy had every right to determine where his girls lived. Plus, Jerry likely knew not to press his luck and incur any potential wrath he had escaped given his family's less than hospitable treatment of Lucille and Dessie Mae.

Life improved dramatically for Lucille when she went to live with her grandparents. In their home, she found loving adults who nurtured her and Dessie Mae. They were still poor but they were cared for as they should have been all along. In those first few days, it was hard for Lucille to know if she could trust what was happening. She didn't know whether they were staying with their grandparents or whether Uncle Jerry was coming to take them back. Would her grandparents treat her and Dessie Mae the same way their aunt and uncle had? After all, she and Dessie Mae weren't their children either. Would she have to continue to hide if she shared her food with her sister? As Lucille managed her uncertainty, she felt that the fact that she and Dessie Mae could eat with the family and as much as they wanted was a good sign.

However, it was her first bath in her new home that thawed her defenses and began chipping away her doubts. When it was time for their bath, Papa Ed brought the metal washtub into the kitchen and partially filled it with water from the well. He then hung up a quilt in front of the doorway before going to the sitting room. (Lucille didn't learn until later that this was to give them some privacy for taking their bath — the same way Mama Liza had privacy for her baths.) Their grandmother had heated a big pot of water and added some of the hot water to the water already in the tub along with something that smelled like the honeysuckle that grew in the yard. She had the girls take off their clothes and sit down in the tub. As the girls began to wash, Mama Liza poured warm water over each girl's head and shoulders. Lucille melted completely and the balminess of the water flooded her with the warmth of her grandparents' care for her. Now she knew she was home; she knew she was safe; she knew she was loved.

There was only one not insignificant hitch to the new living arrangement: when the girls arrived at their grandparents' home, they were not Edward and Liza's only granddaughters under their roof. Their cousin, Elizabeth who was three years older than Lucille was already living there and she had claimed the role of Queen Bee.

"Y'all smell bad," Elizabeth said with a frown and upturned nose on their first day in the house and out of earshot of their grandparents. "Didn't y'all take baths?"

"We took baths," Lucille replied not quite defensively, pulling Dessie a little closer and trying to figure out whether her cousin was making fun of her or just asking a question. Lucille already knew that she and Dessie Mae smelled bad.

"Mama Liza can make your hair look almost as nice as mine but mine ain't as nappy as yours so it might be a little hard. Anyway, you can have one o' my old dresses if you can fit it. You might like it better than that one," offered Elizabeth.

"Thank you," Lucille smiled cautiously, still wondering what to make of the offer and imagining having her hair look almost as nice as Elizabeth's.

"You welcome. Mama Liza say we all gon' be sisters."

Elizabeth's mother, Emma Hatch, Tommy's sister and the girls' aunt, had been seeing a man named Herman Montgomery, a handsome fellow who had a complexion that was so light he could pass for White. He was quite dapper, and despite his reputation as a ladies' man — or maybe because of it — Emma found herself among his many conquests. When she became pregnant, Herman had no intention of marrying her. Emma stayed with her parents and had her child, Elizabeth, in their house. Elizabeth came to know who her father was and, despite his failure to marry her mother, she carried a steadfast devotion to him and, later in life, cherished a family photograph that captured his handsome, well-dressed, almost-White image.

As many Black families can attest, complexions within a family can vary widely — from very light to very dark. Because Emma was brown-skinned — but only slightly so, it was not surprising that a child that she had by Herman Montgomery was very light-skinned as well. Elizabeth also had what folks called "good" hair, meaning it was more naturally like the fine, straight hair of White people and not course, kinky, or nappy as was most Black folks' hair. Like a lot of people of that time — and of today — a number of her relatives were captivated by and adored Elizabeth's light skin and good hair, and therefore, her as well. Through no fault of her own, Elizabeth's aunts fawned over her from the moment she was born, treating her like a prized baby doll and lavishing her with attention.

Elizabeth enjoyed being older but also lighter than her cousins. She knew that asset gave her a higher status and value both among some in her family and in parts of the broader community. She also loved being in the position to introduce the girls to life in their new home. Lucille and Dessie Mae were very appreciative and seemed awed, at least initially, by Elizabeth's confidence, even if she was a bit bossy.

Edward and Liza resolved to raise the girls as siblings and expected Elizabeth to help look after her younger cousins. Yet, they somehow missed noticing the hierarchy she sought to impose. Elizabeth may not have been maliciously motivated to lord her privileges over the girls but she couldn't help being a product of her environment. She was certainly tickled by how "country acting" her cousins were when they arrived.

Lucille and Elizabeth attended school and Dessie Mae joined them when she came of age, although the timing of school varied depending on local needs. The financial conditions and availability of resources of a particular locale dictated when school was held for poor Black children — especially in rural areas. As the school calendar was organized around agrarian considerations, school generally began in the fall after the need for extra hands during harvest time was not as great. All of the children attending their school shared one room with seating organized by age — youngest children sitting in the front and the oldest students sitting in the back.

"Pre-primers, please recite the alphabet altogether," instructed Mrs. Hughes, the school's only teacher. "Primary students, I want you to take out a piece of paper and practice writing the sentences on the board in cursive three times. Beverly, James, Georgia, and Alma, please work on your six-and-seven times tables. Essie, Herbert, Sherrell, Jim and Leon, finish writing your paragraphs on last night's reading."

Lucille loved going to school because it allowed her to discover so many things that she had never thought about, although she never felt entirely sure that she was good at it. She especially liked learning cursive writing and imagined all the things she would write one day. Elizabeth didn't necessarily enjoy school but she was so competitive that she did well enough in spite of her lack of interest. Liza and Edward reinforced for their granddaughters how important it was for them to do their best in school and often reminded them that not long ago it was a crime for children like them to learn to read and write. Uneducated themselves, the grandparents couldn't help with schoolwork but they were vigilant in making sure the girls got their lessons out each night.

Much like the homes the children came from, the schoolhouse itself was subject to the changing moods of the seasons. A late summer that bled into fall meant hot, stifling days with prayers for breezes through the open windows. The teachers allowed breaks for water and brief movement but it was terribly hard for the students to focus with sweat running down their backs. Harsh winters required a steady supply of firewood for the wood stove that heated the room and students rotated the chore of filling the wood box. Even with the heat from the stove, some frigid days forced students to learn in their coats. Lucille thought the worst times of the school year were what folks called "blackberry winters," when cold spurts came in the late spring after the stoves weren't being fired, momentarily dashing the joy and relief of warmer weather.

The girls brought their lunches with them in a shared lunch pail that Elizabeth administered until Lucille and Desi Mae were old enough to be responsible for their own. Their meals usually consisted of cornmeal hoe cakes, leftover meat or fat drippings from the prior night's dinner, any vegetables or other perishables Liza had been able to put up, and produce from their garden when in season.

As they matured, the girls took on even more responsibly around the home. They helped gather eggs, tend the garden, haul water, and bring in wood. Elizabeth, Lucille and Dessie Mae performed some of their chores before school and some after. Once done with the afternoon tasks, they helped their grandmother with preparing dinner if she needed any assistance. After the evening meal, they helped clean up and then worked on any remaining school assignments they had for the next day.

Liza Ann made sure to teach the girls practical skills for taking care of a home. She taught them how to keep the house tidy. They learned how to can the vegetables from the garden. And there were lessons on how to mend clothing and how to sew, first by hand and then on Liza's pedal powered sewing machine. Lucille, more than Elizabeth or Dessie Mae, took to sewing immediately. She didn't even mind the frequent finger pricks of the needle, instead focusing more on completing the garment or item she was working on.

"Slow down, Elizabeth," her grandmother coaxed, "You rushin' through yo' stitches and they comin' out a lil' catey corner. Try to go a lil slower so they even. See how even Lucille's look?"

Of course, Elizabeth took umbrage that Lucille was doing something, anything, better than she was. After all, she was the older and smarter one! Lucille smiled to herself because she loved seeing her work turn out nicely and appreciated by her grandmother. Plus, she didn't mind being better than Elizabeth at something. She might not have been as pretty or as light-skinned as her sister-cousin but she knew she more than held her own in sewing. All of the girls enjoyed quilting with their grandmother. Taking scraps of old fabric and turning them into beautiful quilts that also helped keep the family warm during the winter made them feel happy and proud. Of course, there were bragging rights to be had when one did a particularly good job.

As skilled as she was at sewing and quilting, Lucille's fascination with her grandmother's cooking coupled with her own inquisitiveness resulted in a reputation as an especially good cook as well. Elizabeth and Dessie Mae were decent cooks and the foods they cooked tasted fine. But Lucille's dishes, cakes and pies all brimmed with the care, patience and love she put in them. Try as she might, Elizabeth was a technically good cook but never the virtuoso Lucille would become.

Whatever sibling rivalries may have simmered at home, the girls were a united front outside the house. Elizabeth's sharp tongue could take down anyone who tried to intimidate her sisters. And although Lucille avoided confrontation, she only had to prove herself once as a capable defender if an altercation threatened to turn physical.

"Elizabeth!" called Minnie Jean Freeman, a girl Elizabeth's age, as all the children were finishing their lunches outside. "You think you so cute and that all the boys like you 'cause you high yella and got good hair." Minnie Jean had decided that Elizabeth was too "hinkty" for her own good and getting a bit more attention than she was due. On top of it, Minnie Jean didn't like how well-liked Lucille was by everybody in the school — the teacher, the students, everyone. As for Dessie Mae, Minnie Jean simply didn't like her on general principle, and figured with Mrs. Hughes distracted inside, if she dusted up Elizabeth a little in the school yard, she might knock her down a peg or two and bring a little shame to all three of the girls in one feat.

"Well, Minnie Jean," replied Elizabeth "that's because they do. And if yo' mama combed yo' nappy hair and you washed between yo' legs, they might like you a little better too."

Of course Minnie Jean could not allow such a brazen insult to stand unchallenged. She quickly crossed the few yards between them and pushed Elizabeth forcefully enough that she stumbled backwards to the ground. "You lil high yella heffer!" Minnie Jean yelled. "I oughta beat yo' tail."

Truth be told, Lucille also thought Elizabeth was a little too full of herself at times, but she wasn't about to let Minnie Jean push Elizabeth around. As Minnie Jean basked in what she didn't realize was the short-lived glow of having embarrassed Elizabeth, Lucille casually walked up behind Miinie Jean and using her sizable fist knocked Minnie Jean squarely in the back of her head. Stunned, Minnie Jean was not at all prepared for that. As she turned around to find the source of her attack, Minnie Jean raised her hand to the spot that was throbbing from the unexpected blow. Before Minnie Jean could gather her thoughts or regain her composure, Lucille stepped toe to toe with the bully, faces just inches apart, and said under her breath such that only a few besides Minnie Jean could hear her: "If you ever touch either one of my sisters again, I will stomp a mud hole in yo' lil narrow behind. And if you tell Ms. Hughes I hit you, I will do it twice."

Realizing she wasn't a match for Lucille, who was equal in stature if not age, Minnie Jean backed away rubbing her head. That was the only time anyone ever saw Lucille display any level of violence. After that day, merely balling her fist was enough to remind the boys and girls alike that Lucille didn't play when it came to her sisters.

Liza and Edward's devotion to their grandchildren tied the girls to them and to each other, cementing in the cousins a belief in and commitment to family. Liza's prediction proved true: all three girls grew to treat and love each other as siblings. There were the occasional spats but Liza and Edward didn't brook a lot of squabbling so any real disagreements were left to bubble beneath the surface or out of their presence.

Their grandparents provided a warm, supportive home even in the midst of the prevailing economic and social challenges. Theirs was a poor household like all of the families they knew. With Tommy still providing support, however, the family fared better than many of their neighbors. The grandparents did what they could to make birthdays and holidays special for the girls. Presents were few but Edward and Liza tried to have a sweet or some kind of treat for the girls every now and then.

A reverence for God and faith also characterized life in Edward and Liza's home.

"Dessie Mae, Elizabeth, Lucille, stop the cleaning for now and come sit down," Liza instructed the girls as a sudden thunderstorm broke outside. "The Lord is doing his business."

Lucille never understood why everyone had to be still while "the Lord was doing his business" as indicated by the thunder and lightning that was rioting outside, but she had heard the admonishment enough times to know that all would be quiet in the house until the storm had passed.

Going to church every Sunday was a must. Besides school, church was where the girls could connect with their broader community and other young people their age who lived outside of the Newcastle community. Because their grandparents' kindness and generosity of spirit extended beyond their household, the girls were also able to observe how well-respected Edward and Liza were among their neighbors. Christmases brought the joys and excitements of oranges, nuts and hard candies when their means allowed. On rare occasions, there were gifts of fabric for new dresses, and, occasionally, actual store bought gifts. Even in poverty, the girls enjoyed lives rich in family connection and support and with the security that came from thoughtful, loving parenting. These formative years were consequential for the girls as each would express what she experienced with her grandparents in her own way with her own family in the years to come.

FOUR

Route 1 Box 315
Forrest City Ark.

Dear Grand Son
 Just a few lines to let you here from me I am ok thank the Lord hope you ar two well last week I sent Jackie 5.00 to get some Chicken Wings so this week fare you to get you some Wings if you like them or whet ever you Wount I love you Oh Sarah Day tell yaw she been in school a week and havent got her home in the Board or in the Bad Box love you and you rember me in your Pryers
   love moma leal

Route 1 Box 315
Forrest City, Ark

Dear Grandson
  Just a few lines to let you here from me. I am ok. Thank the Lord. Hope you are two. Well last week I sent Jackie [$]5.00 to get some chicken wings. So this week fore you to get some wings if you like them or whatever you wount. I love you. Oh Sarah say to tell you she been in school a week and havent got her name on the board or in the bad box. Love you and rember me in your pryors.
  love Moma Ceal

In September of 2016, on one of the first mornings after waking up in the vacation home we had just purchased, my wife Juliette and I made breakfast. As we sat at the table, I began playing some gospel music on my phone. It was Sunday after all. The familiar intro to what was at one time one of the most well-known and iconic gospel songs, immediately transported me back to my childhood.

As a kid, my routine on Sunday mornings, after I had cleaned up and gotten partially dressed for church — never fully dressed to guard against spills during breakfast, was to go to the front of the house to help with breakfast, hoping that my father had not already turned on the local radio station playing gospel music. If the radio was not on, I would stop at our family's stereo console in the den and raise the cover which enclosed the turntable, a caddy for cocktail glasses, and a small storage area for a few albums. If the record I wanted wasn't still sitting poised for play, I looked for a white album cover with a large oval picture of sunlight bursting through trees in a forest. The writing in the two most prominent lines at the top of the cover above the picture read "The Edwin Hawkins Singers" in blue and, underneath, "Let Us Go Into the House of the Lord" in a cranberry color. The first track on Side A was "Oh Happy Day."

I. Loved. That. Song. I still do.

Among the sights, smells, and sounds that evoke a powerful emotional response and that can instantly catapult me through time, the song "Oh Happy Day" is definitely one of them. Perhaps it is the pull of nostalgia that takes me to a simpler time in life when I didn't have the worries of being a parent or the cares of paying taxes or the responsibility of planning for retirement. Whatever the reason, I had the same visceral reaction that September morning when it began playing.

The piano prelude with the slightest hint of percussion started the process and as soon as soloist Dorothy Combs Morrison in her penetrating alto sang the first three words of the lyrics "Oh happy day," my body and my spirit responded in an instinctual way. Starting at the crown of my head and radiating down to the center of my chest I felt a chill that ushered a wave of warmth and emotion. As I started to sing along, I couldn't continue for long at all. My voice caught and I got choked up. Tears started rolling down my cheeks. Juliette started crying too and she walked around behind me to wrap her arms around me. We didn't need to say a word: our feelings of gratitude for that moment in our lives were aligned.

To be honest, I get emotional to varying degrees almost every time I hear the song. But this day was different. In addition to the nostalgia the song conjured for me and the instantaneous reflection of my and Juliette's journey in our marriage to that moment, the exponential speed in which the mind works brought me to a remembrance of Mama Ceal and the journey of our family from her life as a maid for over 40 years in rural Jim Crow Arkansas to that day in which her grandson who used to wear sandals made from too small sneakers had purchased a vacation home on Martha's Vineyard with sweeping views of Vineyard Sound. I wondered what she would think and how she might be in awe of this achievement had she lived to see it. I wondered whether she would be proud. For that matter, what would others of our ancestors, for whom property ownership may have seemed almost fantastical, have thought? Had I become the "hope and dream of the slave" that Maya Angelou wrote about in her poem "Still I Rise"? Am I my grandmother's "wildest dream" as the pop culture Internet meme and t-shirt logo proclaim and as a friend suggested to me when I was telling him about her?

Mama Ceal was not born into slavery. However, slavery ended less than four decades before her birth. Although her parents were not enslaved either, her grandparents, my great, great grandparents, had been. I can't fully comprehend the savagery, brutality, cruelty and utter inhumanity that was slavey. There are times I can hardly read accounts as relayed by those who survived it or stand to watch cinematic depictions of its horror. But had I lived during slavery, I wonder whether I would have been someone who had the courage to even think about escaping or participating in a revolt, or fighting for abolition.

When I think of the line from the poem, I wonder what the enslaved hoped and dreamt for. It seems obvious that at a minimum, enslaved persons had to have dreamt of freedom, if not for themselves, then for their children. Freedom from being held as another person's property; from being subject to the whims of sadistic overseers; from rape and the torture of physical and psychological abuse; from the inability to maintain family bonds; from the everyday acceptance of cruelty and brutishness; from the lack of agency over their own bodies; from the denial of their basic humanity.

If that is the baseline for their hopes and dreams, then perhaps I and every other descendant of those who were enslaved in this country represent the fulfillment of those aspirations. But isn't it likely my great-grandparents nurtured similar dreams? While they may not have been enslaved, they experienced the profound inequity of post-Reconstruction, the terror of the Ku Klux Klan and White vigilantes who were determined to limit the ability of people like Mama Ceal's parents from realizing real progress and exercising the rights they should have gained through their freedom. Surely, they still dreamed of being able to provide for their families without the constraint of discrimination and unfair practices that cheated them of equal reward for their labor.

With some distance from slavery, it was inevitable that Black people's contentment with emancipation would give way to frustration with the inequality that made their freedom hollow and paltry. What was the point of being free if they couldn't enjoy the civil rights that they were supposed to have been afforded by the Fourteenth and Fifteenth Amendments? Where was the equality in having to endure substandard ways of living while they watched their White neighbors enjoy a more robust version of life, liberty and the pursuit of happiness? While vast numbers of Black people in the '30s and '40s rose up to protest and march as their children did (and there were many), they certainly harbored the resentment of being relegated to an inferior caste with limited rights and limited opportunities. Like them, my grandmother saw the benefits and privileges that her employers and their children enjoyed. Was it her proximity to their lives that stirred up the idea that her daughter could possibly reach such levels? Why shouldn't her child be able to do what White children were able to do? Whatever it was, something birthed the desire to give my mother the freedom to choose her life and not have it chosen for her simply because she happened to have been born Black, and a woman, in a rural, former slaveholding, Confederate state. Whether my grandmother's dreams were as fully formed as I have imagined, she clearly had a hope for my mother that was rooted in giving her the best educational opportunity that was available to her — even if that meant sending her away to live with and be raised by a relative.

I don't know what Mama Ceal thought of the anxiousness and tension that pervaded the country as America entered the 1950s and 1960s. However, I suspect she could sense that the hope and desire among Black people for better treatment was becoming an even more widespread and urgent expectation. Aspirations and dreams to be allowed simply to survive and to be treated fairly were giving way to demands for the opportunity to reach for lives of abundance and to thrive in ways that were far more common in the White community. Likewise, I don't know if she subscribed to the beliefs among some in the Black community that, to subvert Jim Crow and segregation, one simply had to demonstrate that Black people did not match the stereotypes that had been propagated about them; that through this concept of respectability politics, demonstrating their humanity and civility, Black people could convince their fellow White citizens that they were deserving of better treatment.

One sentiment that was clear in the Civil Rights Movement is that countless people were no longer willing to exercise patience and appeal to the reason and compassion of White America. Those who advocated non-violence and those who supported more forceful means agreed that they had had enough. While many of them did not put their bodies on the front lines of marches, demonstrations, sit-ins, and freedom rides, scores of women my grandmother's age fed, sheltered, and prayed for the younger people who did. These mothers, grandmothers, aunts, daughters and sisters dreamed of the world that their community sought to usher into existence.

My generation came of age in the shadow of the Civil Rights Movement. Despite the gains achieved through the Movement — voting rights and housing legislation and improved, if not equal, access to better educational opportunities, Black people continued to experience discrimination and prejudice. Yet, our parents still dreamed of us taking our rightful places in the land of opportunity that America professed to be. We were taught that until the country lived up to its creed, we had to work twice as hard and be twice as good if we wanted to advance, to "make it." Consequently, many of us did that: we accepted that the deck was stacked against us and worked harder to succeed in our careers and to become examples of the American dream. Yet, we didn't realize that our efforts to shatter glass ceilings by showing ourselves capable and that our determination to give our children the experiences and exposure and access that so many White children seemed to enjoy by right, in some ways, still fed into the dynamic of proving our worth to the dominant White society. We were still dreaming of bringing about a world where our kids didn't have to go to extraordinary efforts to justify their right to simply be and to live their lives without the stress of bias and bigotry.

In the year 2020, after a summer of unrest promoted by the murders of Breonna Taylor and George Floyd, many of us who are descendants of enslaved forebearers allowed ourselves to hope, to dream that a new, enhanced, and more effective dialogue and movement to end systemic racism and all of the other "isms" from which our country suffers was at hand. It felt like we could take comfort that our support of the the work of social justice through our politics, our actions, our giving, and our prayers were finally bearing fruit. We were and are still dreaming.

While I admit, at times, I find my children's generation's impatience with and disdain for attempts to reform "the system" bewildering, I admire and applaud their refusal to accept as status quo the traditional ways of bringing about change. Theirs is a relentless urgency to reshape the norms and mores of society to make it accepting of all people in whatever form of diversity they present. Like many of their peers, my children have a knack for rejecting customs and practices that have — however unintended — promoted disparate treatment and intolerance out of a sense of decorum and politeness. I marvel at how they raise and discuss with their grandmothers topics and issues I wouldn't have dared broach in "polite company" simply because it just wasn't done. It is with that same straightforward candor and expectancy that they prod and shove us all forward in not only acknowledging our shortcomings as a society but also in forcing us to either take a side to which we can devote our energies and support change, get out of the way — or resign ourselves to being relegated to the "dustbin of history." They are dreaming as well, but with their eyes open and their bodies poised to effectuate the change they want to see and to which they believe we all are entitled.

Considering the dreams of my enslaved ancestors, and those of my grandmother, my parents, myself, and my children, it occurs to me that all of these dreams fundamentally represent the same dream: the dream for freedom. In one form or another, we have all dreamed for the freedom from some form of lack or limitation/restriction or oppression or narrow mindedness; a freedom to live without fear the life that we choose, to enjoy equality and the realization of our humanity without oppression, to pursue what makes us happy.

One day a few years ago, I found myself in a profoundly thankful frame of mind. I was thinking of the many things I have to be grateful for. Our family is healthy. We lack for none of the necessities of life. Our daughter was in her last year of law school and I, as proud parent, was anxious to see how she would use her law degree to advocate for the good she wants to see in the world. Our son had left a prestigious job at a global investment bank to intern with an architect in Italy and renovate an Italian villa because it made him happy (and I realized that I wanted him to be happy more than I wanted the cache of being able to say where he worked). And I knew that Juliette and I would be discussing when we were to return to Martha's Vineyard as we continued to work remotely because of the pandemic. Yes; this had to be wilder than the wildest dreams Mama Ceal could have envisioned. It was wilder than the wildest dreams I could have imagined.

To be truthful, it wasn't happenstance that I "found" myself in a grateful mood. A tear was forming in my eye and Dorothy Combs Morrison and that amazing choir led by Walter Hawkins were singing "Oh Happy Day" in the background. After all, it was Sunday.

FIVE

As the years passed, the sister-cousins—Elizabeth, Lucille, and Dessie Mae—grew into their budding womanhood. The differences in their ages had not felt that pronounced until 1927, when Elizabeth turned 15 and prepared for her completion of eighth grade and the end of her schooling, the farthest a Black child could go in the poor rural Arkansas school the girls attended. While she loved her grandparents and enjoyed growing up in the house where she was born, her sights were already set on moving forward with her life and setting up her own house. A few short years later, she would marry Owen Whitley, a quiet, tall, dark-skinned man with broad shoulders who was several years her senior.

"Ooh Lawd! I can't wait to get out of this country and go live in the city away from all these country people," Elizabeth said in a huff as she and Lucille took clothes off the line.

"Mmm hmm," Lucille mumbled, acknowledging Elizabeth's declaration, reflecting her "old soul" and maturity well beyond her 13 years of age.

"I'm gon' have me a husband and a house and we gon' live mighty fine," she continued. "You probably don't understand yet, Lucile, since you so young and just got yo' cycle. Y'all gon' miss me — and I'll mis y'all too — but I will come visit y'all and y'all can come visit me sometimes. And when you come I am gon' show y'all how city folk do."

"I think I understand pretty good," Lucille responded, almost deadpan. "But whatever you do or wherever you go, Liz'beth, I want you to know that I love you and I know you love me too, even when you bein' mean or actin' like you don't."

"Ooh it's gon' be so fine," Elizabeth continued, humming to herself and moving farther down the clothesline to take off a sheet being blown by the wind.

While she didn't expect Elizabeth to respond in kind, Lucille knew Elizabeth had heard her and that was all that mattered. Lucille would miss Elizabeth the most as they were the closest in age and Lucille had watched her navigate the transition to being a young woman. She knew that Elizabeth came by some of her ways through no fault of her own because her aunts and family had made her like that, fawning over her light skin and good hair. Lucille told herself that Elizabeth did the best she could with what she had. Besides, they were family — sisters by choice and love if not parentage.

Dessie Mae, on the other hand, was closest to Lucille and took Elizabeth's impending departure in stride if not a small degree of pleasure.

"Is Liz'beth big? Is that why she want to get married so fast?" Dessie Mae asked her sister.

"Not that I know but I don't think so," said Lucille. "I think she woulda tol' us. You know Liz'beth. She like being in the bright sun with no shadows around her, getting all the attention. She can't help it. Owen seem like a nice enough man and you know she can't wait to be her own boss in her own house."

"I don't know," Dessie Mae chuckled. "She boss this house pretty good." Turning serious, "Are you gon' get married, 'Cille?" Dessie quizzed, obviously wondering about life without her sister one day.

"I don't know. Maybe," replied Lucille. "I don't guess I'd mind it but I ain't in no rush."

When the time came, with no Elizabeth to order them around, Lucille and Dessie Mae were a duo again, but life was certainly better and they were certainly stronger than the last time it was just the two of them.

The impacts of the Great Depression were felt more severely among rural, agricultural, and minority communities, many of which were already indigent and lagging behind the rest of the country. Poor Black families in America were hit the hardest. This was no less true for the Hatch family, one of many hard up families in a farming region in Arkansas County. Even with Tommy's help, as Liza and Edward aged and were less able to work as hard or long, the household struggled.

Because they remained in touch through letters and occasional visits after Elizabeth married, she and Lucille came up with the idea that taking one additional mouth out of their grandparents' house might make things easier for Liza and Edward. The two suggested that Lucille live with Elizabeth for her last year of school as Elizabeth figured she and Owen were in a position to have Lucille. The proposal was a testament to both Elizabeth's and Lucille's love and concern for their grandparents as well as to the strength of their relationship. Though it meant that Lucille and Dessie Mae would be separated, they all agreed that it made sense to help their grandparents in this way and they knew that Edward and Liza wanted Lucille to finish school. So Lucille completed her last year of school living with Elizabeth and her new husband Owen while Dessie Mae remained with her grandparents.

When Lucille finished eighth grade, she returned to live with Liza and Ed and went to work in the fields to help bring more money and help into the household. That she engaged in field work as opposed to some other employment was simply due to the lack of other opportunities. It paid alright and made the most sense.

The speed with which life can change should not have come as a surprise to Lucille given the number of twists and turns she had already experienced in her life. However, within the relatively short span of a few of years, her life would be unrecognizable from anything she could have pictured.

SIX

Returning to the home of her grandparents in 1933 was a smooth and welcome transition for Lucille despite the fact that it was during a time of great economic challenge for her family as well as the rest of the country. Her homecoming reunited her with Dessie Mae, whom she had missed terribly. Going home to the grandparents whom she loved dearly gave her the chance now to try to help them as much as she could. Not only had they been her refuge from a life of neglect and emotional abuse suffered at the hands of her aunt and uncle, but they also cemented for Lucille in both practical and emotional terms, the concept of family. They nurtured her soul and satisfied her longing to believe in and trust family. Lack and hard work were not new, but they were more bearable within the cocoon of the place and among the small circle of people where Lucille came to understand what having a home meant.

The routine in Liza and Edward's house, the chores, the cooking and sewing with her grandmother, relieving her grandfather of some of the outside tasks, the late night whispered conversations with her sister, all brought Lucille a familiar comfort after living with Elizabeth. The rhythm of their life around the house and with the neighboring families in their church were as she remembered. Her grandparents continued to be a big part of the fabric of their community, sharing from their garden and supporting the church's mutual benefit campaigns when they could.

Church potlucks were a common activity among many rural communities during the Great Depression. Not only were the shared meals a source of food for those who had little, they also provided one of the few outlets for fellowship and entertainment for everyone.

It was at one of those potlucks that Lucille first caught the eye of one of her contemporaries: Walter Isadore Eldridge. Walter was the son of Effie Martin and lived with her in Newcastle. His father, Scott Eldridge, lived nearby, but his parents were not married.

Smiling mischievously, Dessie whispered in Lucille's ear as she scanned the lawn of people, "Cille, why didn't you tell me you was co'tin'?" At 16, Dessie Mae was well recognized as the mischief-maker of the crew.

"What in the world is you talkin' 'bout now, silly" Lucille replied, not even bothering to look up from the blonde Jesus on the church fan she was holding.

"I ain't the sharpest knife in the drawer but I think Walter Eldridge sweet on you 'cause he can't stop lookin' in yo' direction every five minutes."

"First off, you 'bout crazy as a Betsy bug. Second off, I don't even know him so I 'spect you got this one wrong lil sister."

"Be that as it may, *big* sister," Dessie replied, "you ain't getting' any younger. So when the time come, don't forget I was the one who tol' you first," concluding her observations with a wink.

Lucille thought to herself that she could barely remember seeing Walter before although she seemed to recall he had a nice smile. As she thought more about it, she did know who his mother was from seeing her at church, though she didn't seem especially friendly. Then she wondered to herself why that crossed her mind or even mattered since there was nothing to her sister's observation: Dessie Mae was just being as crazy as a field lark as she often was. Plus, life had already taught her to temper her expectations.

Walter Eldridge was a solid man of medium height and, unlike his father who was much more light-skinned, shared a dark brown complexion with his mother. A round face, wide-set, intense eyes, a broad nose, and full lips gave him an assertive, handsome look. His brother, James, was light skinned in complexion as well although he had a different father than Walter. Their mother Effie had been disappointed — given her taste in men — that Walter wasn't also lighter in complexion like his father. However, she loved her son and appreciated how hard Walter worked to take care of the family. Since his father did not live with them, Walter and his brother were the main breadwinners for the household, chopping cotton in the summer, picking cotton and working at the local gin in the fall, and doing whatever odd jobs White folks offered.

Regardless, at that point in her life, Walter Eldridge was the least of Lucille's concerns as she was focused on her and Dessie Mae making life easier for their grandparents. Edward still worked the fields to the extent he could, but it was evident that he and Liza were slowing down and Lucille wanted to make sure they were taken care of as much as possible. That is what commanded her attention, not being another notch in the belt of someone she figured was another man-boy trying to prove himself.

In spite of the challenges they all struggled to overcome due to the dire economic conditions, the little community in Newcastle continued to band together and support each other. Times remained tough and the church gatherings offered both practical and emotional support to the hamlet of families. They also provided Walter with the opportunities to interact informally with Lucille and her family. After meeting them "officially," it had taken Walter a while to even get Lucille to engage. She had convinced herself that he couldn't be serious about her and she wasn't going to let herself indulge in some trifling fantasy that there could be a future in spending any time with Walter. Slowly, through building a rapport with her grandparents, he reached a point where he could see that Lucille's opinion of him had softened. From his perspective, it was a great day when she warmed up to speaking with him for more than a few seconds when they crossed paths at church.

"Good morning, Mr. and Miz Hatch. Nice to see y'all. Them sho was some nice tea cakes you made the other week for the potluck, Miz Hatch."

"Hey, Dessie Mae and Lucille."

"Hi, Walter," Lucille managed politely.

"I saw y'all grinning at Deacon Johnson falling asleep this morning," he added to Lucille and Dessie Mae as Liza and Ed had moved on. "I thought I was gon' bust out laughing. Anyway, see y'all next Sunday."

Later, when their conversations had taken on a less superficial tone, Walter asked, "How come you not married yet?"

"I'm not sure it's any of yo' biz'ness but since you asked, I ain't waiting 'round to get married like some o' these girls," Lucille responded, trying to conceal the smile his question prompted. "Marriage ain't no plaything to me. If I find a good, kind man who likes me and I like him, then maybe I will. But I ain't got no time for someone who think they gon' treat me like one o' they hogs or run 'round on me like a bunch of these knucklehead mens be doin'."

In her response, Lucille had shocked herself more than Walter. She wondered where all of that had come from or why she had said it out loud. How did she get to a place of speaking so freely when more often than not she was being chastised by Dessie for not speaking up for herself and being encouraged by her grandmother to actually say what she wanted instead of deferring to everyone else?

Undeterred, Walter continued, "How will you know if you done foun' a good one?"

"I'll know. He'll show respect to his family and to me and mine. He'll be somebody I like as my friend not jus' my husband. He'll want to have some chil'ren and work hard fo' his family. He'll know ain't nothin' mo' important than family."

"I would never boss over you or run around on you," Walter ventured.

"Naw, I don't think you would."

A year and some change later, on December 30, 1935, Lucille and Walter married. Of course, Dessie Mae was happy to remind Lucille of her prediction although she was sad that her pal and protector was now no longer going to be next to her when it was time to go to bed at night and their whispered conversations would come to an end. The family was pleased as Dessie Mae, Elizabeth, Tommy, and her grandparents all felt that Walter was a decent man.

Marrying Walter meant that Lucille would leave Edward and Liza's home and move into the home that Walter shared with his mother. The new house wasn't far from her grandparents' place but it wasn't as well situated as the one she left. It was difficult to get to the Eldridge house because it was located through a ravine. The road leading to it was one of the worst in the area. It was all but impossible for a motor vehicle to go anywhere near it and wagons swayed and shook violently trying to navigate the way. The sides of the road were extremely steep and only those who knew well the passageway and where they were going ventured down it after dark, and then only if they absolutely had to.

Unfortunately, the reward for risking the hazardous route was even more discouraging on more than one level. The house itself was in bad shape even for those times: it was drafty and had an old, inefficient, and unsafe wood stove to heat it. Walter had done what he could to shore it up, but there were still holes in the floorboards and, like most of the rural houses in the area, had no plumbing at all so an outhouse was the only means for relieving yourself and water had to be carried from a spring and stored in a cistern.

To make matters worse, Effie quietly fumed that Walter's marriage to Lucille dashed any hopes she had of him giving her light-skinned grandchildren. It took many years for her to forgive Lucille for visiting that disappointment upon her. While not completely hostile to Lucille, Effie was decidedly cool to her.

"Are you gon' have some dinner, Ms. Eldridge?" Lucille asked her mother-in-law.

"No thank you," Effie replied. "Yo' beans a lil salty fo' my taste. I'll have me some of them greens I made in a bit."

"These beans ain't salty, Mama," Walter interjected. "You should try some."

Had she been less confident in her cooking, Lucille might have questioned how she could have made such a simple mistake. But she knew her beans were not, in fact, salty, and knowing how much Walter liked her cooking, Lucille ignored the slight and ate with her husband. She appreciated the narrow line he walked to be respectful of his mother and also take up for his wife. Besides, she knew Effie ate her fill of any leftovers when she thought Walter and Lucille wouldn't notice.

"Yo hair sho look pretty for church, Lucille," Walter effused, complimenting his wife as they were preparing to leave.

"That's interesting," volunteered Effie, "I'm surprised that balm worked on yo' hair since it so much coarser than mine."

"Mm-hmm," Lucille replied to acknowledge she had been spoken to. "It worked just fine."

At times, it was almost comical since Lucille had known what real mistreatment was; Effie's insults and slights never quite hit the target as intended.

"Louise, hand me that jar over there on the table," Effie directed at Lucille. "Oh, I'm sorry," she chuckled, "That ain't yo' name."

Despite the challenges — financial and interpersonal — Lucille was content in making her home there with Walter. She had come to love her husband as much as for who he was as for the patience he showed in wooing her. He hadn't played the ladies' man when she didn't immediately return his interest. She had taken her time in letting him in and he had been willing to allow her that time. She had watched him carefully and saw that, unlike some of the other fellows in their area, he hadn't felt the need to strut or prove what a big man he was. He worked hard to care for his mother and keep their house going. And Lord knows, he was patient with his mother's occasional antics.

During their courtship, Lucille had also been vigilant for any signs of meanness or ill temper as she never forgot the treatment she and her sister suffered as children at the hands of their relatives. Walter had succeeded in showing her that he was someone Lucille could trust and build a life with, someone with whom she could share her dreams of a big family. True to her nature, despite her resolve to not expect too much of life, she continued to look for the best in situations and people — including her indifferent mother-in-law. She knew Effie wanted the best for Walter even if she wasn't sure that that was Lucille.

But what made Lucille love Walter even more was that they confided in each other and shared their innermost thoughts and secrets. Despite his outward confidence, he had been willing to share with Lucille what scared him — something no man had ever done in front of her.

After filling out his draft card, he often worried that he might be called to war, leaving Lucille alone with his mother, whom they both knew wasn't easy to get along with and didn't appear likely to warm up to Lucille anytime soon.

"I ain't no pitiful lil' baby," she told him as they whispered in bed, careful not to wake his mother. "If you have to go to war, what you need to worry 'bout is coming home to me. I can take care o' myself and yo' mama — even if she don't want me to." She smiled to ease his tension. "Besides, ain't no talk of another war so you best go to sleep 'cause you got to meet that mule in the mo'nin'."

Other times she had to let him just get out what he had bottled up inside and then try to calm him using whatever reasoning might soothe him in the moment.

"Sometimes, when I be comin' home late at night, my chest get tight worryin' that you might want to leave me 'cause you ain't happy here with me in this raggedy shack."

"Walter Eldridge, have I tol' you I wasn't happy? I'm plenty happy right here next to you. Besides, I done put too much sweat in this old house to leave it fo' some other woman to come in here and enjoy," she chuckled, nudging him with her elbow to underscore her teasing.

"I heard the Klan over the way been making a lot of noise lately. What you gon' do if some o' these crackers just kill me fo' sport. I ain't scared for me, I be scared I won't be here to take care o' you."

"The good Lord gon' take care o' all o' us, Walter. Sho, you got to be careful, but don't be frettin' yo'self over that," she would tell him, this time invoking God as the charm. She loved being able to comfort him and help ease his mind when he got worried.

Those first years were particularly hard. Walter continued to do field work and work at the cotton gin when the seasons permitted. He also began sharecropping on a parcel of land owned by the Horton family, one of the landed White families in the area who also owned the gin and a small general store in Newcastle. Lucille continued to work the fields until the grip of the recession began to lessen. As the economic recovery eventually began to reach rural communities like Newcastle, Lucille was able to hire herself out as a washerwoman, washing and ironing for some of the White families in the area whose financial conditions had also improved. Seeing how a couple of those families lived only cemented Lucille's dreams of having a family of her own and giving them some of the things she had glimpsed in those homes.

It took some time before Lucille's dreams for a family to be realized. Perhaps it was the backbreaking work she and Walter performed that delayed their plans. Perhaps it was the disapproving glare of a mother-in-law who had not fully welcomed Lucille into her home that locked her womb. Perhaps it was the stress of the extended financial uncertainty or the random threat of violence they could never ignore that did not allow her body to entertain conceiving. Whatever the cause, the couple went childless for more than five years after they married.

SEVEN

In October of 1941, just months prior to their sixth anniversary and the United States entering World War II, the couple welcomed a baby girl. When asked where she got the name "LaRuth," Lucille told people that she heard it from one of Walter's friends and liked it. The truth was she read the name in the newspaper about a bank robbery but she didn't feel the need to share that piece of information. The important thing was that her dream of having a family of her own was coming to fruition.

Walter was thrilled to have a daughter but the demands of his need to work and support the family meant that he saw very little of her during the week. It was even worse during ginning season as late nights at the gin were frequent. Although he was gone a lot, Lucille knew that Walter was much more attentive to his daughter than her father had been towards her. Lucille stayed with her baby for a couple of weeks to regain her strength, nurse the baby, and get her somewhat settled, but she had to return to work if the family was to get by.

Walter's mother Effie's indifference to Lucille extended to LaRuth as well — at least initially — such that when Lucille went back to washing and ironing, she left LaRuth with the Winfreys, an older couple who were friends of the family and who lived near them instead of with Effie. Ironically, although he was not a regular presence in his son's life, Walter's father, Scott, adored little LaRuth, and visited her when he was in the area. As she grew to be a toddler, Scott was sure to have some kind of treat for LaRuth whenever he came.

Lucille could not contain her joy in watching LaRuth grow. And she loved loving on her child in a way she herself wasn't. Her feelings of love were soon joined by worry, worry for the kind of future she could give her daughter and the kind of life LaRuth would have. She wanted more for her, more than Lucille had been able to carve out for herself, and more than her limited education had offered. She desperately wanted a different path for her daughter.

From Lucille's perspective, the little school in Newcastle was only slightly better than the one-room schoolhouse she had attended as a child. There was more space that allowed the children to be divided up a little better by age and grade but the resources and quality were clearly not as good as the Negro school in Forrest City, the nearby town where Elizabeth lived.

Forrest City was named for Confederate General Nathan Bedford Forrest who had built a commissary in the area and was instrumental in building a railroad that connected to the Memphis-Little Rock Railroad. Forrest is also known as the first Grand Wizard of the Ku Klux Klan.

By the 1940s, Forrest City had long enjoyed a water and sewer system, electric street lights in much of the town, and many paved streets. The intersection of the Memphis & Little Rock Railroad and the St. Louis, Iron Mountain & Southern Railroad at Forrest City had made the town a hub for local farmers. An industrial plant established by the city had welcomed Forrest City Machine Works, where Elizabeth's husband Owen worked, enabling him to secure a modest home for himself and his wife. While the recovery from the Great Depression was slow, the end of World War II ushered economic growth that certainly took hold in Forrest City well before it reached Lucille and her neighbors in Newcastle.

Forrest City also had the largest Negro school for miles. Lucille was certain that attending that school and the opportunities it could offer were what she wanted for LaRuth. She was clear on this point. What was also clear, however, was that she and Walter could not afford to move to Forrest City as they were just getting by as it was. Notwithstanding the fact that there was no money to move or find a new place to live in Forrest City, she had no idea what she or Walter might do even if they could move there. Maybe she could be a maid but that really wasn't her preference if she could help it. It was more than a notion to deal with some of the women she washed for. Besides, Lucille knew Walter did not want to leave his mother even though his brother wasn't too far away. The only real option as Lucille saw it was to have LaRuth go to live with Elizabeth so that she could go to the better school. That way her daughter could at least have a chance at the life that Lucille saw her White customers living but that she couldn't even dream of for herself.

Although they had been struggling with the idea for a while, Walter and Lucille didn't come to a final conclusion until after school had started in the fall of 1947.

Elizabeth and Owen were well into their marriage for over 20 years at this point and any hopes of having children had long since died. It wasn't surprising then that Elizabeth leapt at the idea of having a child in her house. She felt that she could now share all of her learning and "city refinement" with someone she could mold to appreciate it. Lucille knew Elizabeth might be a lot to take, but felt that LaRuth's being around Elizabeth's occasional haughtiness was a small price to pay for her daughter to take advantage of that better Negro school and to have the chance to secure for herself a better life. While she appreciated it might be hard at first, Lucille could not begin to imagine the real cost to herself or LaRuth of having her daughter go to live with her persnickety sister-cousin Elizabeth.

With the decision made, Lucille and Walter explained to LaRuth what a great thing it was to be able to go live with her Aunt Elizabeth and Uncle Owen and go to the nice school in the city. They didn't do so to get her agreement. Things were already settled as far as they were concerned. Moreover, they knew that LaRuth was not old enough to be able to decide what was best for herself. But Lucille hoped that her daughter might be able to understand why she was sending her to a better school and the better opportunities that came with that. Unfortunately, Lucille's hope was in vain as LaRuth didn't understand or appreciate what it all meant. All she knew was that she had to go away.

"Now I want you to be a good girl and mind Elizabeth, you hear?" Lucille admonished her daughter.

"Yes ma'am," a quiet LaRuth replied.

"You gon' have so much fun at yo' new school. And it's gon' be plenty of little girls and boys for you to play with."

"Can Jesse Winfrey go to that school, too?" LaRuth asked. Jesse was one of the Winfrey's grandsons who was LaRuth's age and her favorite playmate.

"Naw, baby. Jesse Winfrey gon' stay and go to school out here. Everybody can't go to the special school like you gon' do. You'll see Jesse Winfrey when you come back out here."

"Then maybe I can just stay here and keep going to school with him?," LaRuth ventured hesitantly, realizing even at almost six that she was approaching a line she was not to cross. She couldn't dispute her mother.

"Naw, baby girl. You gon' go to the school in Forrest City but I know you gon' like it. Just wait and see," she said, gently squeezing LaRuth's brown cheeks between her thumbs and forefingers.

With that, LaRuth understood that there was no further conversation about where she was going to school. She had already figured out that leaving Newcastle not only meant she had to leave her parents, whom she was starting to miss already, and her grandmother whom she had not considered she might miss. It also meant leaving behind Jesse and the entire Winfrey family, her extended family with whom she was extremely close, and the second home where she had spent so many days running and playing and so many nights when her parents were working late or just because the Winfreys wanted her to stay over.

If there was anyone who loved LaRuth besides her parents, it was the Winfreys. LaRuth wondered how anyone could think this was a good idea if she had to be without her mama and daddy *and* the Winfreys. Neighbors Alex and Erin Winfrey were more like grandparents to LaRuth than Effie.

Alex Winfrey worked the fields and at the gin like Walter, and his wife Erin stayed at home tending house and watching other folks' children while they worked. They were a bit older than LaRuth's parents which is why they felt more like grandparents to her. The family didn't have any daughters so they loved having a little girl to fuss over as one of their own. To LaRuth, the Winfrey boys felt like her uncles or big brothers, all of them were older than she was, and they treated her like a prized niece and little sister. The two oldest sons had already moved out of their parents' home. Both lived nearby, one with his wife and the other with his wife and two sons, one of whom was Jesse, LaRuth's partner in fun and with whom she spent the most time playing in Newcastle.

"Did I see you had LaRuth up in that tree playing with those other little boys?" Erin playfully asked her grandson.

"She can climb real good, Big Mama," Jesse answered his grandmother. "I was right there to make sure she wasn't gon' fall."

"LaRuth! Were you up in that tree with them boys?" she quizzed, continuing to tease them both.

Nodding her head vigorously and unable to suppress a face-covering smile, LaRuth replied "Yes, ma'am."

"Well y'all better be careful. She ain't no rough and tumble knucklehead like you boys!"

Adding to the anxiety of leaving her family was the fact that LaRuth hardly knew her Aunt Elizabeth and Uncle Owen. She had not spent much time around them other than at family funerals or infrequent gatherings and she had never been to their house before. On top of it all, her mother had told her repeatedly how nice their house was *and* how particular Elizabeth was about her things *and* how careful she had to be not to break anything or make a mess. These lessons her mother couldn't seem to stress enough. But the day had finally come and here she was in this new house that was to be her home away from her parents and all that she knew and valued.

For Lucille, the first night that LaRuth went to live with her sister-cousin was not the first night she had spent away from her daughter. LaRuth had spent many nights with the Winfreys, but none of them had felt as significant nor had any evoked the feelings Lucille was experiencing now that LaRuth was actually gone. What seemed like perhaps one of the longest nights of her life began well before the sun had set; it started the moment the car pulled away taking her only child to Forrest City. She and Walter did not have a car so another relative had agreed to come out to pick up LaRuth to take her to Elizabeth. The sound of gravel crunching under the car tires and the tears in LaRuth's eyes that wouldn't fall opened a place in Lucille's heart that was instantly filled with sadness, longing and . . . was this perhaps jealousy? No, she couldn't spend any time dwelling on this.

"Fix your face, Lucille," she thought to herself. They had agreed that this was the right thing to do and that was all there was to it. LaRuth had not cried when she left and Lucille refused to let the fact that she already missed her baby girl elicit any tears on her part. She might spend the night crying but her weeping at this moment was only happening deep inside her breast.

For LaRuth, there was no way for her to know then that this new house she was coming to would be the first of three residences that she would share with her aunt and uncle. It was a small house by most standards but it was much larger and a bit scarier than the one LaRuth shared with her parents and grandmother. It had two bedrooms, a bathroom inside the house, a small eat-in kitchen and a small living room-sitting area. It was on a street with other similar houses and you couldn't feel any air blowing in like the old house. The new living arrangement also offered LaRuth a room of her own — not that she wanted one — instead of the small space on the cot her father had made for her and that sat in the corner of the room where her parents slept in the house in the ravine in the country. Her Aunt Elizabeth's house wasn't a lot to the casual observer, but to the scared six-year-old, it suggested that her aunt and uncle must be rich beyond imagination compared to her mother and father. She had never seen Colored people with such a nice house.

Nothing about this place reminded LaRuth even remotely of the home she had left. It was so neat that she worried that she might be messing up something just by standing in it. As her mother had alluded, LaRuth soon learned firsthand that her Aunt Elizabeth required near absolute cleanliness and that everything had to be in its assigned place. Actually, this was worse than her mother had warned. Where life with her parents had been engaged and easygoing, her new life was going to be much more subdued and regimented. LaRuth's clothes had to be neatly pressed whenever she went out. She would be taught the ways of acting like a lady and carrying herself modestly. Loud outbursts and exuberant laughter were frowned upon. While she didn't know any of these things on that first day, something in her spirit, the uneasiness she felt, was warning her of life to come.

Although she may not have understood fully what was in store, she could see the stark differences that were right in front of her face. Besides the house itself, the furniture looked like the new furniture she and Jesse had seen in the Sears catalog and that they dreamed of buying for their mothers one day. There was no smell of her father's work clothes that had been washed in lye soap; no fragrance of the Mum deodorant that her mother used on Sundays; no odor of smoke from a wood stove, and no hint of the heavy swampy musk of the ravine. In fact, other than the faint scent of Uncle Owen's cigarettes that burned her nose a little, there did not seem to be much of a smell at all.

The newness of the house, the fact that it was so sterile, the lack of any familiar objects to which she might anchor herself were all too much for her little soul to take. Even though she had promised to be a big girl, she couldn't stop the flood of previously stubborn tears from streaming down her face or the sobs that she tried to keep anyone from hearing after her Aunt Elizabeth put her to bed.

EIGHT

Route 1 BX 315
Forrest City Ark

Dear Grand Son,

Well I rec, your Card thank you fare the Pretty Card and fare you thanking of me Will Balter gave me 52 lins and Serah Grease my noise John & Donna had a Birth day Dinner it was good and a Pretty Cake, 9 Corse it was my 73 year I thank the Lord fare it also fore my Daughter and my lovely Grand Childrens I love you all So much all is ok. You be a good boy Oh When did you Say you Would go And where I am tryeng to get the enguator to make you Some Brownies So drop me a nate & let me know. Bam Bam Say Hi and fare you to be a Sweet Bay because they love You two Will you be a Sweet Boy I Love you and your family

love Moma leal

Route 1 Box 315
Forrest City, Ark
Dear Grandson
 Well I rec. your card. Thank you fore the pretty card and fore your thinking of me. WEll Baxter gave me 52 liks [licks] and Sarah grease [greased] my noise [nose]. John & Donna had a birthday dinner. It was good and a pretty cake of course. It was my 73rd year. I thank the Lord fore it. Also fore my daughter and my lovely grandchildrens. I love you all so much. All is ok. You be a good boy. Oh when did you say you would go and where. I am trying to get the the engretin [ingredients] to make you some brownies so drop me a note & let me know. Bam Bam say hi and fore you to be a sweet boy because they love you two. Well you be a sweet boy. I love you and your family.
 love Moma Ceal

I like to think that I share a kindred spirit with my grandmother. I try really hard — with varying degrees of success — to emulate the generosity, kindness, loyalty, and humility that she exhibited. In fact, I probably fail much more than I am successful. But in this instance of like minds, I refer to something altogether different, something less altruistic. I'm considering the fact that in spite of generations of conditioning, we both chose dark-skinned spouses.

 I met Juliette Williams on the first day of law school at Georgetown University. She came into the large lecture hall and walked to a seat in the row in front of me. I was already seated with two other guys I had met earlier. She was wearing a business suit and carrying a briefcase. When she got to the spot she had selected, she turned to the three of us, introduced herself, extended a handshake, and then turned around and took her seat. The three of us looked at each other, stunned by how composed and self-assured she was. In quick, whispered comments, we agreed she was a serious student and had it all together. Thinking to myself, I was convinced she had to be older as she came across so much more mature and ready for the world than I felt at the time. And although she was a beautiful woman who was indeed impressive, confident, stylish and outgoing — and as I later learned smart, funny, and generous — I had quickly assigned her to the category of women who would be my friend since she didn't fit my "type."

 Fortunately for me, Juliette and I did become friends, very good friends. It was through our friendship that I came to know her as someone who was intellectually curious, not afraid to share a contradictory point of view and who challenged traditional, familiar, and/or lazy beliefs. I also found her to be a truly thoughtful person who shared her concern freely.

One day sitting in class, I realized I was too distracted and could not pay attention to anything my torts professor was saying. I decided to take a break for a few minutes and go sit outside to clear my head. Within a few minutes, Juliette had come to sit next to me.

"Hey, how are you?" she asked.

"Oh. Hey" I replied. "I'm fine. Just needed some air."

"Are you sure?" she prodded. "You were rubbing your stomach just now in class. You do that when you are anxious or worried about something. And you tend to say you're fine as a reflex. How are you really?"

I was stunned. In my head, I'm thinking "What the hell? Who is this person who has paid so much attention to me that she has figured out when I'm anxious or worried — and that I rub my stomach when I am? I didn't even realize I did that!"

Up to that point, we had indeed become great friends. We shared similar outlooks about life. We were both very close and committed to our families. We both saw our faith as essential components to who we were. But it wasn't until that moment — the moment that I realized that she really saw me — that I think I considered our relationship could be more than platonic. It was the moment that I realized that I could fall in love with her. It was her ability to go beyond the surface and truly see me that caused me to look beyond the superficial to see her, eschewing the lessons of colorism I had ingested. She forced me to confront the influences impacting how I had constructed what my "type" was and that were impeding my ability to truly see her.

We have an ongoing discussion among my wife, my children and me. It centers on the inconspicuous way — separate and apart from the obvious ways — the construct of race, racism, and the aftermath of slavery affect — and infect — how people see themselves and others. Juliette likens it to living in smog that you have to navigate every day whether or not you leave the confines of your home. I like the notion of "smog" but I've come to think of racism less like the smog, which you can see, and more like an indiscernible kind of pollution. Or better yet, more like carbon monoxide — invisible and odorless but potentially deadly. In this instance, imperceptible though omnipresent.

The writer Alice Walker is credited as the person who first used the term "colorism," according to Lori Tharps, Associate Professor at Temple University.

Walker defined colorism in her 1983 book *In Search of Our Mothers' Gardens* as "prejudicial or preferential treatment of same-race people based solely on their color." Professor Tharps provides an insightful explanation and exploration of colorism in her own book, *Same Family, Different Colors: Confronting Colorism in America's Diverse Families*. While colorism exists in many countries and cultures outside of the U.S., I'm focused on the U.S. flavor as seasoned by slavery and that impacts Black people in this country.

While there are numerous ways slavery has colored — pun intended — the world view of its Black (and White) descendants, the concept of colorism may be one of its most insidious. It induced Black people to turn one of the tools of White supremacy and racism against themselves. Using a system among enslaved people that arbitrarily valued lighter complexions over darker ones was one of the ways to create divisions among them. Lighter skinned "house slaves" enjoyed the benefits and privileges of more frequent bathing, more and better food, often from their masters' tables, and better clothes than those who worked outside. In contrast, "field slaves" were often darker in complexion and generally the subject of much harsher treatment in terms of the difficulty of the labor required of them and someitmes even the types of punishments they were subjected to. The success of the system was not only to make Black people believe that there was in fact a qualitative difference between them based on whether they had lighter or darker skin but to do so in a way such that they weren't even aware that they had internalized this concept or able to see how they continued to perpetuate these self-destructive ideas.

There is a famous quote by Carter G. Woodson in *The Miseducation of the Negro*, the book that chronicles his study of this and similar dynamics as relates to the indoctrination of Black people:

> *When you control a man's thinking you do not have to worry about his actions. You do not have to tell him not to stand here or go yonder. He will find his 'proper place' and will stay in it. You do not need to send him to the back door. He will go without being told. In fact, if there is no back door, he will cut one for his special benefit. His education makes it necessary.*

Black people were taught that it was better to be "more White," i.e., more like White people — and by logical extension, less like Black people. Thus, it is not surprising that among many early Black social clubs and organizations, membership hinged not on educational or professional attainment or on moral character, but instead on whether potential members could pass the "paper bag" test. (That is: whether their skin complexion was as light or lighter than the color of a brown paper bag.) Even some churches and colleges are said to have used the paper bag test to determine membership and admission.

This desire to be more White also led many Black people to abandon their own stores and merchants post integration in favor of the previously segregated institutions as a sign of their success and an exercise of their new freedom. Demonstrating an ability to afford to shop where White people shopped or engaging in the kind of social activities that had been seen as "White" activities was a sign of social status and affluence. The satirical phrase "the White man's ice is colder" reflects a realization that some Black people patronized White establishments solely because they were White-owned and not because they were necessarily better.

While there are and have been many Black people who had the awareness not to perpetuate the concept, none of them could escape the day-to-day impact of it, because it permeated — and continues to permeate — our society. The idea has been reinforced in innumerable ways: the prevalence of white and light-skinned figures in children's toys and books; negative characteristics attributed to dark-skinned people; the pay gap that exists between lighter and darker skinned people; and the harsher treatment of darker skinned people compared to their lighter skinned counterparts in the criminal justice system. Although it has improved significantly, it was much more common to see models and actors in commercials, print ads, TV shows and movies who were light to medium brown-skinned than ones who are dark-skinned.

My grandmother was only one generation removed from slavery. Although her father and mother were not born enslaved, her grandparents and some of her aunts and uncles were. Thus, it would not be surprising that she felt the direct impacts of the "slavery mindset" that tethered her immediate family to slavery. Similarly, it would not have been unusual or unexpected if she held beliefs that favored light over dark skin. Should Mama Ceal have been given a "pass" if she did in fact hold views based on colorism since she was so close to the events and institutions giving birth to colorism? If so, does that intuitively mean that those of us who are more generations removed from slavery bear greater responsibility for perpetuating it?

Although Mama Ceal's mother was light-skinned, her father was not. She took on the pigment of her father, while her younger sister, Dessie Mae, though not as light as some in their family, was closer to their mother's complexion. I am not aware of specific incidents of mistreatment that my grandmother suffered as a child because of her dark skin; however, I do know that she witnessed first-hand the preferential treatment that her "sister-cousin" Elizabeth enjoyed because of her lighter skin. Did Mama Ceal question her value as a result of the smog she lived in? Did she ever wonder what she could or had a right to expect from life compared to Elizabeth and other lighter skinned Black people? Did she even consider that she was beautiful given her dark skin?

Her mother-in-law had preferred that her son, Walter, my grandfather, choose a light-skinned wife so that he could ensure having lighter children, closer to his father's complexion than his own. While some tension between a wife and her husband's mother may be inevitable, at least some of the strain in her relationship with her mother-in-law was due to the fact that my grandmother wasn't likely to be able to give her mother-in-law light-skinned grandchildren, since both she and Walter were dark-skinned.

Just as her mother-in-law feared, the child my grandparents produced, LaRuth, my mother, was not light-skinned, though not quite as dark as her mother and father. Lucille adored her child and didn't appear to be the least bit concerned about her color. Nevertheless, like her mother, LaRuth grew up with the same smog of colorism that impacted her sense of self in numerous ways. When Lucille sent LaRuth to live with her Aunt Elizabeth so that she could attend a better school and have access to a "better life," did she somehow communicate that a better life was associated with Elizabeth's lighter skin?

As early as elementary school, my mother learned to temper her expectations because she was aware that she was a dark-skinned child. Although she was a smart girl, dressed tidily, and had respectable home/family support in her aunt and uncle, she knew that her darker skin imposed certain limitations. Like everyone else, LaRuth's teachers lived in the smog as well. When selecting students for starring roles in school plays and holiday pageants, the teachers' colorism compelled them to choose light-skinned students time and time again for prominent roles. Ultimately, my mother came to accept that being a member of the chorus or supporting cast was how things were for her. Of course, I am tempted to question how much this impacted my mother's thinking. However, the counterpoint to that idea is represented in an old photo from her high school prom. Her boyfriend and date at the time was darker than she was. Still, it's not impossible that colorism influenced her thought. Did my father's complexion play a role in her attraction to him given that he was light-skinned?

How did the color of her skin impact what she allowed herself to hope and dream for? How did she feel about the fact that both of her children shared a lighter complexion than she did?

Which brings me to me. Unlike my grandmother, I was most definitely influenced by colorism. I took to heart the admonitions from family members to be careful not to stay in the sun too long in the summer for fear of getting "too dark." I believed that worse than being called "too black" (and therefore ugly) was to be called "African," as it suggested a double negative of being dark and "uncivilized." Being a product of TV, I cheered for Tarzan when he vanquished the evil African cannibals (and for the Western cowboy when he shot each murderous Indian). I consumed — even if not willingly and knowingly — everything Hollywood and Madison Avenue were selling. And the girls who I liked were always invariably light-skinned like the ones I saw celebrated on TV and in magazines and in movies. Throughout grade, middle and high school, the objects of my first crushes and the authors of my first heartbreaks were light-skinned girls. In fact, by the time I had reached college, I remember thinking how odd it was that a fellow freshman, a girl I had met within the first few weeks, was the first dark-skinned girl that I had really fallen for. However, even after that initial point of awareness, with only a couple of exceptions, I continued to buy into the image being hawked by advertisers and marketers and found myself attracted primarily to light-skinned women. Unlike Mama Ceal though, I am several generations removed from slavery. Does that make my vulnerability to the smog of colorism more or less understandable?

The lottery of heredity gave Juliette and me two children, our first-born, a dark-skinned daughter, and a second-born son who is lighter skinned than both of us. Being the progressive Black parents that we strived to be, we embraced our heritage, our Blackness, giving both children African middle names. As the first child and grandchild for our respective families, our daughter enjoyed a childhood that celebrated her beautiful brown skin and natural hair in addition to her being the first. We bought Black books, toys, dolls, computer games and music. We decorated our home with Black art and ensured she saw the beauty of being Black in all that surrounded her. We wore and dressed her in African and African-inspired clothes. Her home displayed Black nativities for Christmas; her Christmas list was shared with a Black Santa; and her Christmas tree showcased decorations with ornaments featuring scenes with Black carolers and Black elves and Black angels.

Despite these conscious efforts to build a strong, self-confident Black child, she still lived in the smog, the carbon dioxide of colorism that we could not shield her from entirely. She has since shared as an adult that it was only after leaving her private, predominately White, independent school experience in Washington, D.C. and attending a large public magnet high school in Chicago with a broad array of Black and brown and other diverse children that she felt "beautiful." Needless to say, we were shocked but even more saddened. Damn that smog! It had still overpowered our intentional efforts to shield our beautiful child.

Our community continues to struggle with the issue with many of us still oblivious as to how much we have ingested the deleterious effects of slavery. Yet, awareness grows. My own evolution in admitting and tackling how colorism impacted my way of thinking and seeing gives me hope that others can do the same. My children's generation gives me even more hope. I wonder is it because of or in spite of (or some combination of) compounded eras of thought and struggle that my grandmother's great grandchildren seem to have healthier and more self-aware approaches to how they think about color, how they consider the way society treats people of varying colors, and how they work to be and make others mindful of the privileges society affords varying groups of people? Their generation's fearlessness and fortitude in confronting dangerous, antiquated ways of thinking like colorism encourage me. They ways they speak openly and uncompromisingly about social and cultural phenomena like what it means to "be Black," that previously have been taboo, inspires me. They give me hope.

I doubt my grandmother held any regrets around how she navigated the smog of colorism. I'm grateful that she did not contribute to the smog by saddling my mother or our family with misguided thoughts around valuing lighter skin more than darker skin on top of all the other messages we were getting to do so. I am also grateful that, before she died, my grandmother had the chance to meet and know Juliette. I like to think that part of the reason she adored her as she did was that Mama Ceal saw herself in Juliette — dark skin and all.

I also like to think that Mama Ceal sees the way that I continue to try to navigate the smog of colorism in a way that hopefully dilutes its potency even if only a little. I hope she is proud.

NINE

At long last, Elizabeth would know what it was like to have a child in her house. Notwithstanding her excitement to finally have a little girl to raise, Elizabeth's many years without children had stunted her ability to understand what was most important to them. In addition to her challenge in appreciating how to nurture a little girl, Elizabeth was especially buttoned up and firm in her bearing as she embodied her impression of a married lady living in the city. Her early years as the prized baby to her aunts also contributed to the straight-laced, rigid and stodgy person consumed with being a model representative of the race that she had become.

In Elizabeth's mind, a good home, warm meals, clean clothes, and concern for LaRuth's education were the best way to show her love for her new "daughter." There was most assuredly a very definite way that things should be done and Elizabeth would make sure that LaRuth knew it. Her approach was to be a strict disciplinarian to ensure that LaRuth was raised "right" and trained to be a proper young lady. She was not going to have anyone in the family saying that LaRuth turned out bad because of how Elizabeth had reared her. No, sir! She had enthsiasticaly embraced the Bible's teaching that if you "spare the rod" you spoil the child. The cumulative effect was that despite her best intentions to love LaRuth the best way she knew how, her parenting would almost always be a little less than what LaRuth needed.

Unfortunately, as she assumed the role of mother, Elizabeth did not understand the importance of little hugs for no reason or licking cake batter off the mixing spoon or bare feet in damp grass after a rain shower or adding a bit of sugar to the cornbread just because. Surprisingly, however, even though she was not nurturing by nature, she did have the presence of mind and enough empathy to realize that sleeping in the room with LaRuth for a few nights after her first night of barely audible crying and whimpering might help her adjust to her new home a little better, a rare demonstration of maternal warmth and understanding.

On the morning of her first full day in her aunt and uncle's house, LaRuth awakened to the smell of bacon that accompanied the grits and eggs that Elizabeth was making for breakfast. The biscuits weren't as good as her mother's, but they didn't taste bad. This was not the bowl of oatmeal or Cream of Wheat that became her standard breakfast, but this was LaRuth's first day with them and Elizabeth wanted that first meal to be nice. After eating, Aunt Elizabeth, as LaRuth would call her, showed LaRuth how to clean the table and the kitchen and to wash dishes. What followed seemed to LaRuth like a long list of instructions, including where to put away her clothes, how she should keep her room, how to help clean the rest of the house, and how to mind her manners — in addition to an even longer list of prohibitions.

"LaRuth, you have to let the water get hot before you rinse dishes so it kills the germs but don't stick your hand under the faucet or you'll get burned."

"When you fold the towels, fold them in half this way and then over two times."

"When I call you, I want you to answer 'Coming' and start walking to me right away, understand?"

"Always wash your hands when you come from outside."

"Don't touch Owen's cigarettes."

"Don't touch the radio. It's not for children."

"Don't leave your clothes on the floor when you take them off. Fold them and put them away in the chifforobe or in the hamper."

"Don't talk or chew with your mouth open."

"Don't nod your head. Answer with 'Yes, ma'm' and 'Yes, sir' or 'No, ma'am' and 'No, sir.'"

"No singing at the table."

Elizabeth had already made plans for her daughter to attend the Colored elementary school. Although she should have been placed in the first grade given her age, LaRuth started the new school in the "Pre-Primer" level that met every day from 8am until noon. The teachers didn't know what she knew already so they placed her in the lower level to see what she could do. By the next term, she was placed in the more advanced afternoon Primer group and moved to second grade instead of first when she started the following school year.

Elizabeth walked her to school in the mornings and went to retrieve her at noon during the first few weeks of school. After that, LaRuth was allowed to walk to and from school with the other Pre-Primer children and their parents who lived on her street and who Elizabeth knew from the neighborhood. Other than those walks home from school, Elizabeth was very protective and didn't allow LaRuth to play outside much. Most of her play was in the house, pretending to cook for her doll using Uncle Owen's ashtrays as her dishes. After several more weeks of successfully walking to school and back home with the neighborhood children, Elizabeth relaxed a bit more and allowed LaRuth to play outside with the other children but limited to their yard and sometimes in the vacant lot next door.

The only other entertainment in the house when LaRuth arrived was the radio that Elizabeth listened to daily. She didn't follow the latest songs but she did listen to the news and kept up with her soap opera, *Stella Dallas*. LaRuth could listen too as long as she didn't appear to be paying too much attention or taking too much interest in the story. One day when Elizabeth was distracted and didn't turn off the radio at the conclusion of that week's episode, music began to play. The unusual phenomenon of a popular song playing in the otherwise staid residence coupled with the cheerful melody of the tune must have sparked something inside LaRuth. Without thinking, forgetting herself, LaRuth started dancing with an exuberance and joy she hadn't felt since moving to Forrest City.

It didn't last long.

"My lands!" Elizabeth exclaimed. "What in the world do you think you are doing?"

LaRuth froze in mid motion, realizing instantly that she had done something very wrong, incurring her aunt's profound disapproval.

"Do you think I'm raising you to be some two-bit hussy shaking her behind like a hell-bound heathen?"

LaRuth guessed correctly that she wasn't actually supposed to answer.

"I don't know what you may have done before, but we don't do that in this house. Respectable young ladies don't carry themselves like that. Besides, White folks think that's all Negroes want to do anyway — shuffle around and shake they behinds. Well, no ma'am. We are not doing that here."

LaRuth couldn't figure out what was worse, the embarrassment of being seen dancing or the intensity of Aunt Elizabeth's disapproval. If she could, she would have shrunk into the tiniest speck of dust and let herself be blown away. Since she couldn't do that, she shrunk her expressiveness instead and wrote in stone, deep in her heart that not only shouldn't she dance but that she wasn't any good at it anyway. She adhered to that lesson for the rest of her life, dancing only in instances where she absolutely had to because she couldn't avoid it, like a couple of slow dances at her prom and years and years later at her son's wedding.

If ever there was a textbook example of the adaptability of children, LaRuth's quick acclimation to life with Aunt Elizabeth and Uncle Owen very well may have been it. She made herself as compliant and as inconspicuous as she could, following Aunt Elizabeth's rules of the road for the most part. She spoke when spoken to, was exceedingly polite in her manners, and learned to display contentment regardless of her true feelings. She missed her parents; she missed Jesse; she missed the ease of life in the country. But there was no point in telling anyone or showing how she felt. She anticipated plenty of lectures about how fortunate she was and how appreciative she should be such that there was no need to invite extra ones. The pretense seemed to work as all her aunt could see was a very well-behaved, mannerly, respectable child who didn't sass adults the way she had seen other children who clearly weren't being raised right do.

During that first year, although she didn't get to spend Thanksgiving Day with her parents, she did get to visit them that weekend and even got to see Jesse and his family while she was there. To her surprise, although she hadn't asked for anything, there were Christmas presents for her in her Forrest City home — ones that she actually liked: a new doll and bubbles that she was allowed to blow — but only outside. She also got to spend several nights with her parents while school was out for the holiday.

Lucille presumed that LaRuth was just happy to see her and Walter to explain the extra tight hugs LaRuth gave her when she came home. She failed to appreciate what a true escape and opportunity just to be free those early visits were for her daughter. Or perhaps she couldn't bring herself to consider that her daughter might be more than a little unhappy. Even something as simple as playing cards or being able to laugh at good natured teasing made those visits everything for LaRuth. Lucille could not see and LaRuth could not explain how cutoff from her mother and father she felt.

Yet, it was the fact that she was cut off from her parents that spared LaRuth weeks of anguish and grief but also delivered to her a bombshell that forever changed her life and that of her mother.

TEN

Occasionally, Walter made time for a Saturday night out with some of his friends who lived nearby. Saturdays were usually the day of choice since Sunday was the one day of the week when they didn't have work obligations and there ws nowhere to go except church. Lucille didn't mind him going out with his buddies as he didn't do it often and he worked hard for their family. She had no interest in going but figured he deserved periods to laugh and have a drink with the other men.

Such was the case on a Saturday night in February of 1948. Walter and four friends, Joe Willie Himan, Nods Lane, Ocie Lee Siggers, and Leon Sims made their way to a Forrest City juke joint as they had done several times before. They parked a car along the river at a spot near their homes and crossed the river by boat to save time and money. When it was time to go home, they made their way to a small store on the east side of the St. Francis River where they had left the boat. Although he had reluctantly joined the crew for the trip in the boat earlier in the evening, Leon was afraid of boats and the river. His fear had gotten the best of him at the point it was time to go home and he begged off joining them on the return trip. Instead, he paid someone to drive him home even if it was the longer way. Just as midnight approached, after a bit of good-natured teasing that they would be home in bed by the time Leon got home, Walter and the three other friends bid Leon good night and headed home as they had done many times before.

Although the men had had a few drinks, no one had drank more than any other time that they had gone out and none of them were drunk. There was nothing unusual about the evening as it had gone as many others had before.

Until now.

At some point in the middle of the river crossing, the boat they were using flipped, dumping all four men and their only lantern in the water. The hour was completely dark. The men were far from both banks. The water was murky. The cold of winter, bitter. Walter and his friends met staggering challenges as they tried to first right the boat and then, after abandoning it, to swim to the banks. Perhaps had it not been a freezing night, they might have had more tolerance to battle the river's current. Perhaps had there been a brighter moon, its light might have given them a better sense of direction to swim toward the shore. Perhaps had it been spring, summer or fall, when they were not encumbered with winter coats, they might have been better able to tread water long enough to get their bearings and find the riverbanks. However, on that night, too many factors fought against their desperate efforts at survival. The pitch blackness disoriented the men; their waterlogged clothes burdened them; the frigid temperatures paralyzed them; and the muddy water overtook them.

As Leon neared home, he saw that the car was still parked where they had left it and knew right away that something was wrong. When he went to the houses of Nods and Joe Willie and found that they weren't there, his fears were confirmed: the men had not made it across the river. Neighbors were called into action and began to search by boat, foot, and car along both sides of the river.

Lucille knew immediately that the knock on the door of their little house in the middle of the night portended no good. The news of the group's disappearance left her reeling. Like the family members of the other missing men, she hoped against hope that they had made it to one of the banks and were trying to get home. When the boat was found down river from where the men had attempted to cross, the families and search party realized that theirs had become a recovery effort instead of a rescue mission. That day turned into days, which turned into weeks. Authorities dragged the river for several days but rivermen suspected that the cold temperatures kept the bodies submerged. The local paper ran an article about the tragedy and included information that a $10.00 reward had been offered for the recovery of the bodies.

A couple of weeks passed before Walter's body was found. During that time, LaRuth was completely unaware that her father was missing and presumed dead. On the day she found out, LaRuth had walked home with some of the other kids on her street and come in to put her things away per her prescribed routine. Elizabeth was busying herself over the stove and called LaRuth to her. Interrupting her cooking, Elizabeth walked over to LaRuth and put her hand on the child's shoulder.

"I'm sorry to tell you this, dear, but your father is dead. He drowned. We are going to the services on Saturday."

She gave LaRuth what amounted to a hurried, loose and uncomfortable embrace. Both unsure what to do next, Elizabeth directed LaRuth, "Go change your school clothes," and awkwardly turned back to her cooking.

The day of the funeral was a blur for LaRuth. She, Aunt Elizabeth, and the Forrest City contingency who were driven by Elizabeth's half-brother, Elporter, were late, and the service had begun when they arrived. LaRuth was brought to her mother who drew the child close with a kiss on her forehead and a hug. But Lucille was also mindful of trying not to disrupt the service by calling too much attention to themselves. LaRuth wasn't sure of what to make of the efforts to create space for her next to her mother since other relatives had all but completely filled the rest of the front pew. A more astute observer might have gathered that it seemed that those in charge had not remembered that there was a child of the deceased in addition to his other relatives. That observation was lost on LaRuth as she was more concerned about being next to Lucille. Leaning on her mother and soaking in the comfort of her embrace, LaRuth mostly stared at the coffin and felt the vibrations of her mother humming, sometimes along to the music of the choir and sometimes when no singing was happening at all.

LaRuth closed her eyes when it was time to lower the coffin into the ground in the little cemetery behind the church. She couldn't see that her mother had done so, too. LaRuth could barely think of her father in the wooden box, but it was too hard to watch it going into the ground. She wished that she could have seen her father one last time, but she didn't ask. Not until many years later would LaRuth learn that the undertakers and family had all agreed that an open casket was not advisable in light of how badly the body had decomposed being in the water for so long.

LaRuth could not understand why everyone seemed so happy at the repast. The abundance of food that people had brought and the lively conversations and laughter that overflowed from the church didn't fit with how sad she felt. She stayed as close to her mother as she could for as long as she could. However, Lucille had to greet and accept the condolences of the family and neighbors who were there and also take in the reunion of so many family members that she hadn't seen in such a long time. LaRuth would have asked to at least spend the night with her mother but Elizabeth had already explained to her before they left Forrest City that it didn't make sense for someone to have to come back to get her on Sunday since she was to be in school on Monday. As a result, she found herself holding on to her mother longer than usual when it was time to go but refusing to shed the tears the onlookers with their expressions of pity seemed to expect.

Once everyone had left, Lucille spent the evening in a state of despondency. She now found herself in a home with a mother-in-law whose son was dead and who had never fully accepted her. What was to become of her? What was to become of LaRuth? She should have spent more time focusing on LaRuth during the few hours she was with her. Why hadn't she thought to tell Elizabeth before they arrived that she wanted LaRuth to stay with her that night? Even though LaRuth hugged her tightly, she didn't ask if she could stay. Had LaRuth wanted to leave? Lucille wondered if being in Newcastle made LaRuth too sad? Did LaRuth prefer to be with Elizabeth more than with her?

That night, LaRuth was much more successful at hiding the tears that lulled her to sleep. She really didn't want Aunt Elizabeth joining her in bed. She felt better holding herself and imagining that she was still under her mother's arm feeling the music pulse through her. What she couldn't know was that her mother was doing the same, holding herself while grieving the loss of her husband and the separation from her daughter — and hoping she was doing the right thing by having LaRuth live with Elizabeth.

ELEVEN

Following Walter's death, Della Horton, the wife of Lee Horton whose family owned many acres of area farmland, the cotton gin and the small general store in Newcastle, asked Lucille if she wanted to come work for their family as their maid. Some folks presumed that was the Hortons' way of being helpful since they thought well of Walter and he had been a good worker for them. When she considered it later, Lucille laughed to herself that Mrs. Della didn't say it like she was asking. But it didn't matter. Lucille knew it was her decision to make and she knew her mind: she wanted — no, she needed — something else to occupy her, so she willingly accepted the offer.

The job came with her own room and Lucille was happy to escape both from the house she had shared with Walter and from living with his mother. (Lucille knew Effie was hurting too but she had to make this change. She vowed to herself to visit and check on her mother-in-law.) The room was attached to a small barn and had been built for a farm hand. It was airtight, unlike the little house in the ravine, and she didn't have to worry about precarious trips to the outhouse like before; there was one just behind her room. Lucille imagined this room as a nice place for LaRuth to stay with her when she came to Newcastle on her breaks from Forrest City.

From what she knew of them, Lucille felt the Hortons were decent enough as far as White people went, perhaps better. They seemed generally respectful toward Negroes and she noted that, while they sometimes slipped, they didn't talk to her as if they were speaking to a child the way most White people did. Although Lee Horton appeared stern, Lucille came to appreciate his wry sense of humor. Della Horton enjoyed being the wife of a successful business owner and loved hosting her Bible study group and the local chapter of the P.E.O. Sisterhood, a women's organization founded in 1869 and that promoted philanthropy to support educational opportunities for women. Lee and Della Horton were staunch pillars of the local Methodist church and were, by all accounts, a quite prominent family.

Working for the Hortons meant handling all of the cleaning and cooking for them, working at Lee's brother's house down the road one day a week, and also providing houekeeping help to Lee and Della's son and daughter-in-law, Eugene and Marian, whose house was closer than next door as it shared space on the Horton property. Eventually, she also helped take care of the Hortons' grandsons, who were born several years later. Managing the care of three houses wasn't easy but Lucille was accustomed to hard work and after several months, she had developed a number of routines and strategies to make her tasks more manageable. Even with all the work, this job didn't feel as onerous to Lucille as having to go from house to house to collect and deliver washing and occasionally having to haggle with some of the housewives about how much she was due a particular week. As far as she was concerned, it was a heck of a lot better than spending hour after hour in the fields. With steady pay, she could buy a few nice things for LaRuth and do some things she wanted to do for herself. Her growing sense of independence brought a little joy to what had felt like a season of not much more than gloomy day after gloomy day.

Although it took her a few more years than her mother, LaRuth also developed a greater sense of independence, even as she navigated the web of her aunt's protocols. LaRuth's move to middle school also came with a move to a different house with Uncle Owen and Aunt Elizabeth. The people who owned the one Owen and Elizabeth had been renting moved back into town so the Whitleys and their charge had no choice but to find a new place to live. The new house was similar to the last with two bedrooms, a bathroom, a slightly larger kitchen and a living room. LaRuth had her own room again and this time she didn't need the comprehensive orientation of rules and instructions. She was already a master at cleaning the house, helping with laundry, and keeping her room tidy.

Employing the technique that had worked at home, LaRuth was a similarly compliant, obedient student. Her teachers saw her as a child who clearly had good home-training and a quiet, capable student who was smart but not remarkable. That suited LaRuth just fine.

It hadn't taken much for LaRuth to figure out that she wasn't likely to be picked for starring roles in the programs the students performed for their parents or as a queen or a lady in waiting in the royal courts for the holiday pageants. Those parts went to her classmates with much lighter complexions. She and the other dark-skinned students made up the chorus and were given supporting minor parts. Besides, blending into the background was easier and came with fewer disappointments once you got used to it.

If she hadn't already learned the lesson to not put herself in a position to be disappointed, it was reinforced for her the one time she attempted to step out of the shadows into the foreground. Her physical education teacher had noticed that she was a really good basketball player. She didn't showboat and didn't need the limelight but was a solid team player and responsive to coaching. He told LaRuth he wanted her to consider joining the girls basketball team, an idea that excited LaRuth.

Mustering up as much courage as she could, "Aunt Elizabeth?" LaRuth questioned after dinner one evening and while helping get the dishes washed.

"Yes?" Elizabeth replied.

"Coach Turner says that I'm really good at basketball during PE. He says he wants me to play on the girls basketball team. I think I would like to play. May I join the team?"

"That's nice, LaRuth, but basketball isn't really for young ladies" Elizabeth explained.

"Yes ma'am. But it's a girls' team. And I am really good."

"Yes; I know it's a *girls'* team, but those girls aren't being raised to be a respectable young lady like you are. I don't believe playing on the basketball team is a good idea. Tell your coach 'thank you' but that I said 'no.'"

"But —"

Interrupting before LaRuth could say anything else, Elizabeth concluded the conversation, "Now that's all I am going to say about that. Watch your mouth and don't talk back or you will be going outside to get me a switch. You understand?"

"Yes ma'am"

Elizabeth didn't disclose to LaRuth that she had heard rumors that another of the coaches was having sex with some of the female students. From Elizabeth's perspective, that was not an appropriate topic to discuss with a child. In refusing to give a reason, she further cemented LaRuth's feelings that as long as she lived in her aunt's house, her aunt arbitrarily controlled her life.

Because he had left the child-rearing to Elizabeth, Owen did not intervene in any of her decision-making. However, he tried to make life a little easier for LaRuth in ways that he could. A clandestine piece of candy every now and then or an occasional invitation to ride to the store were part of Owen's ways to take the sting out of Elizabeth's strictness. LaRuth might not be allowed to play basketball but he figured some months later that there was no reason he couldn't take her to see the Harlem Globetrotters.

Of course, LaRuth was excited to go. Everyone knew the Harlem Globetrotters were in town. It seemed to LaRuth that almost all of the kids at school were talking about it and planning to go. She hadn't let on to anyone that she was going too but she could hardly wait. It must have been the excitement of the rare outing that caused her to forget to put away the pajamas she had left folded on the bed the morning of the game. Upon her return home from school that afternoon as she changed and put away her school clothes, Aunt Elizabeth called out to her from the kitchen — "Come here, LaRuth."

"Coming" LaRuth responded as she immediately started moving toward the kitchen.

"Where are your bedclothes supposed to go after you get dressed in the morning?"

"In the chifforobe," LaRuth replied, wondering why Aunt Elizabeth was asking such a question.

"Well, if you know where they belong, why didn't you put them there this morning before you left for school?"

LaRuth wondered if this was one of those questions she wasn't really supposed to answer.

"Cat got your tongue?" asked Elizabeth. "This room looked like a pigsty when I came in here before I left for work this morning. I know I've told you time and time again how you are supposed to keep this room and take care of your things. Haven't I?"

"Yes ma'am" LaRuth replied, feeling a knot growing in her stomach and thinking to herself that the room couldn't have been a pigsty since her pajamas, if anything, would have been the only thing not in order when she left that morning.

"I don't know why you can't seem to listen and do like I ask," Elizabeth continued. "Well, staying home this evening and thinking about it is probably what you need to do instead of going out to some basketball game. Maybe next time you will remember to do your chores like you are supposed to and not disobey me as you did this morning."

The "but" and any other words of argument were swallowed before she could open her mouth. LaRuth knew it was pointless to try to explain or convince Aunt Elizabeth to change her mind. She would have to hear about the Harlem Globetrotters from the other kids.

At least she didn't have to be embarrassed as well: none of the kids at school expected her to go anyway.

TWELVE

As difficult as it often was, LaRuth's time in Forrest City wasn't all bad. She had a ready friend in her cousin Gerdene Hatch. "Dene," as she was known to everyone, was LaRuth's cousin because Dene's grandfather, Moses, and LaRuth's grandfather, Tommy, were brothers. The two girls were the same age and in the same grade. While Aunt Elizabeth didn't allow LaRuth to go to other children's homes to play, she did let her play at Dene's house and allowed them to spend the night with each other occasionally. The two weren't best friends but they were close and enjoyed spending time together.

In addition to her trips to visit her mother in Newcastle, LaRuth had other opportunities to escape the stifling atmosphere of Elizabeth's house. During the summer, she got to spend time with her mother's sister, Dessie Mae, who lived outside of Forrest City, in Caldwell, which wasn't quite as far as Newcastle. Just as Lucille had loved Dessie Mae's wit and spirit as children, LaRuth loved the times she could visit with her Aunt Dessie. Added to the bonus of offering a much more relaxed atmosphere, Aunt Dessie could always be counted on for a joke or two at Elizabeth's expense.

"We not going to church today, okay?" Dessie said to her niece.

"Yes ma'am," LaRuth smiled to herself at the thought of missing service, an occurrence that happened only if someone was truly ill in Aunt Elizabeth's house.

"Don't you mention it if 'Lizbeth don't bring it up, you hear? Every now and then we need a break. Plus, the rest of us ain't as holy as she is, pootin' perfume."

Time at Dene's house also offered brief respites from Aunt Elizabeth's cloistered household. Dene's mother, Aunt Lizzie, reminded LaRuth of her own mother from her physical appearance as she had darker brown skin and was more full-figured than was Aunt Elizabeth. Like Aunt Lizzie, the family's house was much more relaxed and comfortable. LaRuth could breathe more freely and feel less like she was about to do something wrong or break something.

Dessie Mae and Lizzie didn't pay too much mind to Elizabeth's "persnicketyness." Truth be told, they didn't even fault her for it as they knew she had been indulged as a child. They knew Elizabeth usually meant well even if she did have the clumsy habits of appearing to look down her nose at her cousins and acting much too prim and proper for anyone's liking. Lucille, Dessie Mae, and Lizzie all took Elizabeth with a grain of salt, an extravagance LaRuth could not afford because she was a child and because Elizabeth was essentially her "second mother."

In addition to outings to see her mother and Aunt Dessie, and the time she spent with Dene and Aunt Lizzie, it was the unexpected gift of friendship that provided LaRuth with perhaps her strongest source of support and means for surviving the stern environment in which she lived.

One afternoon, a few months into her second-grade year, LaRuth walked alone amongst the group of kids who trekked home from school. Cloaked in her adopted shyness, LaRuth wondered what chores awaited her after her math tables and spelling homework were done. She hoped that her shoes didn't look too scuffed up as to merit a comment from Aunt Elizabeth.

LaRuth had grown comfortable speaking little and living inside of her head, another coping mechanism to shield herself from undue attention and disappointment. Because she was both on the younger side of the group of kids who walked home together and able to fade into the background, she was spared the teasing that some of the kids experienced. Most days passed with little fanfare other than the occasional joning among the older ones or someone playing the dozens. Only this day would be different as she found herself jolted out of her internal conversation.

"Hi. I'm Liz. Well, actually, Elizabeth. Elizabeth Franklin, but I go by Liz. I know you're LaRuth" a brown-skinned, slightly gapped-tooth smiling face said to LaRuth. "Miss Elizabeth asked my mama if my sisters could watch out for you when we all walk home. You're quiet, ain't you? Want to be friends?"

While Liz possessed the same formal name as LaRuth's Aunt Elizabeth, a fact LaRuth found so odd given Liz's disposition, no one called her anything but Liz. Besides the name and a genuine devotion to LaRuth, the two Elizabeths had almost nothing in common. For as much as Aunt Elizabeth was serious, muted, and stern, Liz was lighthearted, bubbly, and cheerful. She had a spirit of adventure and made LaRuth laugh. The two were so devoted to each other that a casual observer might mistake them for sisters even though Liz had sisters of her own, including one who was within a year's age of her and LaRuth and in their same grade.

Despite her approval of the friendship, Elizabeth maintained the rule of no overnights at each other's houses. It didn't matter though; Liz and LaRuth were already joined at the hip — and the heart — so sleepovers weren't needed to cement their relationship.

When LaRuth got her period, it was Liz who was the first to comfort and reassure her. Neither Lucille nor Elizabeth had allowed themselves to realize that it was becoming time to have a conversation with LaRuth about the changes her body was to undergo. Afraid she had done something wrong, LaRuth initially tried to hide this development from her aunt. When her best friend confided in her, Liz convinced LaRuth to tell Miss Elizabeth. Once informed, Elizabeth immediately tried to be helpful and even seemed to LaRuth to feel bad that she hadn't talked to her before it happened.

After Elizabeth started working as a nurse's aide, she allowed Liz to come home with LaRuth occasionally so that she wasn't always alone until Elizabeth arrived. It helped that Liz was a good student as well and the girls were sure to do any homework. Besides, Elizabeth had instructed the neighbors across the street to keep an eye out for LaRuth and report anything and everything they saw going on at the house.

"Mrs. James should have picked you for the mistress of ceremonies," Liz consoled her friend. "You read the best to me."

"Thanks, but I didn't think I was going to get it anyway. Plus, I don't know why they make everybody read for these programs if they are going to keep picking the same people," LaRuth added, knowing that her friend understood the implication.

"You mean the same *light-skinned* people," Liz interrupted, taking the opportunity to underscore the point.

"Uh-huh. But we don't have to worry about messing up in the back," LaRuth replied. "Besides, the chorus might fall apart without us."

"Girl, do you think we can be famous as professional chorus members?" asked Liz posing for the imaginary photographer. "I bet you Lena Horne started out as a chorus member."

"Nope," replied LaRuth. "Look at her. I'm sure her 'Mrs. James' made sure she was the MC of every program."

The friends laughed to themselves as they finished their lunches and prepared to return to class.

Elizabeth knew that the neighbors, other members of her family, and even Owen thought she was too strict with LaRuth. She could see the barely concealed mockery behind their polite smiles. She wasn't blind. She saw how Owen tried to pal around with LaRuth. But she owed no one an explanation and she refused to give any of them the satisfaction of knowing she cared what they thought. Her vow and obligation had been to God once He decided to bless her with the chance to be a mother. She held fast to her unspoken promise to LaRuth and to Lucille whether they knew they wanted it or not: to make LaRuth into a model young woman prepared for life in a world that none of them had made and that would not be particularly kind to her.

It was as clear to Elizabeth as it was to anyone else of the time, Negroes did not get a fair shake. If a lack of fairness were all there was to be concerned about, she perhaps could have relaxed a bit. However, her life and the lives of every Negro person she knew was contingent upon how they navigated a society that was not only frequently hostile to them but also patently dangerous. Negro women had an even harder time given the way women were treated in general. Just as White women were less than White men, Negro women were less than Negro men, and both were less than even the lowest White person. She knew that though LaRuth looked like she might grow into an attractive young woman, she did not have light skin or fine hair like Elizabeth so LaRuth was going to have a harder time making it. She had to be smarter, cleaner, more respectable than others if she was to achieve a level of progress in life that Elizabeth felt LaRuth should have — and that would also prove to everyone what a good parent Elizabeth had been.

Elizabeth had seen what happened to Negroes who weren't prepared or willing to accept their place. They were made examples for others to see the consequences; they were taken advantage of, beaten, raped, burned out or lynched. The only real option that she could see that might give LaRuth a chance was to raise her to hold herself upright and act like she had some sense and home training, like a respectable young woman. Maybe then she could be somewhat safer and make something of herself.

She loved this child she had been trusted to raise but there was no way in Hades she would send her into the world unprepared or allow her to turn out like some of the loud-talking, bad mannered, "low-class" members of the race who further reinforced the negative images and stereotypes of Negroes, those ugly, distorted perceptions that influenced how White people saw her and her family. No; she could not add to that image with this child. She intended to show them all what Negro excellence looked like and ensure that her daughter was respected as one of the best of the race. Elizabeth was certain that excellence could not be achieved by excessive coddling and allowing lapses that others might consider minor to go unaddressed. It was better to be disciplined at home by people who love you than to have to be punished in the streets or worse — in prison — by people who didn't.

Most importantly, Elizabeth was determined to give LaRuth a life that Elizabeth herself longed for, one in which she could be self-sufficient without being dependent on a man to provide for her. She knew that she was not going to let herself resort to the menial labor or domestic jobs to which most colored women were restricted. She would see to it that LaRuth would not have to pursue such a life either. In that aspiration, Elizabeth and Lucille were aligned even though they had never articulated it to each other. What if LaRuth could go to college? Maybe she could be a teacher! Wouldn't that be something? Yes, Elizabeth thought to herself, if that could happen, even White people would have to acknowledge that her daughter was a credit to her race.

THIRTEEN

Route 1 Bx 315
Forrest City Ars.

Dear Walter.
Oh it was so good to talk to you I am so glad you is turn ok. well I hope you get the Chicago Job. I know you dont weunt to stay at Caroline But that you can see them Some time well Balter callen Bone were Braken So he all tape up he can go to School after he see the Hacton Monday every one eals is ok only the teachers give Serah to much home werk to do She here david talk about his home work so she have Sometuo you be sweet and dont fare get to Pray and go to Church I love you
                    Moma Ceal

Route 1 Box 315
Forrest City, Ark

Dear Walter,
Oh it was so good to talk to you. I am so glad you is durn ok. Well I hope you get the Chicago job. I know you dont wount to stay at [your Aunt] Cardlene but that you can see them some time. Well Baxter coller bone were broken so he all tape up. He can go to school after he see the Doctor Monday. Everyone eals is ok only the teachers give Sarah to much homework to do. She here David talk about his homework so she have some two. You be a sweet boy and dont fore get to pray and go the church.
I love you
Moma Ceal

When I tell people that I am from the South, I often get the response: "But you don't have a Southern accent." If Juliette, a native New Yorker, is around, she will laugh because she can always hear it. She also appreciates that it may be a situation when I am being careful to suppress any accent. My response to the comment is usually that I, in fact, do have one and that the person should hold their opinion until they hear me on the phone with my mother or late at night when I'm tired.

In work settings and even some social ones, I, like many Black people, am hypervigilant to speak clearly, to enunciate each syllable and each word carefully, to be more clipped, and to be more demonstrative in conveying my engagement. Somehow, somewhere in my journey, I learned that this way of speaking and presenting was vital to being viewed as professional and to accessing opportunities for advancement. My "professional" voice has been curated with such care over so many years that sometimes I slip into it without even realizing I have.

It is not uncommon for someone in our family — or any Black family for that matter — to walk into the room while someone else is on the phone and then, without having heard any of the substance of the conversation, ask the person on the call when they have finished: "Was that work?" The unspoken but mutually understood context for the question is that the person on the phone was using a voice that the other person recognized as one used for professional, more formal settings or when talking to someone who is not Black.

The phenomenon is called "code-switching." The dictionary definition of code-switching refers to alternating between two or more languages within the context of a single conversation, for example, the way native Spanish speakers in the United States switch between English and Spanish when talking among themselves or the way the patrons and proprietor of a Polish deli in Chicago slip in and out of Polish idioms.

However, a 2019 *Harvard Business Review* article entitled "The Costs of Code-Switching" defines code-switching as "adjusting one's style of speech, appearance, behavior, and expression in ways that will optimize the comfort of others in exchange for fair treatment, quality service, and employment opportunities." From this more contemporary perspective, the term has taken on a broader meaning to capture the practice among Black people (as well as other people of color and people who find themselves members of minority groups in a society) of modulating and/or changing the way they speak or act depending on the context or situation.

An argument can be made that most people have the desire to be accepted, to "fit in" in whatever environment we may be. Because humans are tribal, this practice of socially adapting to our environments has likely existed forever, whatever our tribe happens to be. In academic environments, we act in a way to demonstrate our intelligence — or at least hide our ignorance. If caught in a sports conversation at a social event or business meeting, those without real knowledge or interest feign an understanding or appreciation so as not to stand out. It is not rare to hear stories from women, gay, differently-abled, left-handed or anyone else whose identity places them in an identifiable sub-group who have changed the way they deal with those in the dominant group.

However, few groups have had as much riding on the line if they "get it wrong" as have Black people. For a Black person, failure to code-switch — to modulate a natural confidence, an expectation of equitable treatment or an assertive tone — can have huge consequences, fatal consequences. That Harvard Business Review list of what might be viewed as benefits obtained by code-switching should be expanded to include "survival."

There is a temptation to view code-switching as a more recent phenomenon; yet, the ability to read the everyday, potentially volatile situations when interacting with White people that characterized life for Black people in the US — and particularly in the post-slavery Jim Crow era — was critical. As my grandmother grew into young adulthood, there is no question that she would have had to know that there was a way she had to carry herself, a way she had to talk, a way that she had to defer when dealing with White people. Those restrictions had to have been magnified in her role as a maid. In addition to being Black and a woman and having to observe the rigid racial and patriarchal caste system she lived in, her very job required her to be subservient and deferential to her White employers.

There is no shortage of cinematic depictions of "sassy," or "uppity" Black women who reaped disastrous consequences because they didn't change the way they acted in front of White folks or because they didn't conform to the prevailing requirements of their caste. Think Leslie Uggams' portrayal of Kizzy in *Roots*. One of the most gut-wrenching scenes in the television miniseries occurs when Kizzy is loaded into the wagon of her new owner, Master Tom, after she was sold because she dared to learn how to read and write and had used those skills to write a pass to help an enslaved man run away. Consider the plight of the character Sophia, played by Oprah Winfrey in the movie *The Color Purple*. Sophia is beaten senseless and placed in jail for having the audacity to fail to show appreciation when the White mayor's wife, Miss Millie, compliments Sophia on how "clean" her children are, and not only indignantly replies "Hell no" when Miss Millie asks her if she wanted to be her maid, but also fights back when the Mayor slaps her for her disrespect. Or consider the indignity experienced by Viola Davis' character Aibileen in the movie *The Help*, when she was admonished to use a separate bathroom from her White employers. Even though I believe that my grandmother's employers of over 40 years treated her fairly, especially compared to others of the time, I cringe when I imagine that scenes like these were likely all too familiar for her as either happening to her or to people that she knew.

I can recall one instance in which I noticed Mama Ceal seemingly acting differently when White people were around. It was one summer when my sister and I were spending several nights with her. A White couple, Mr. Robert and Ms. Helen had come to visit the Hortons, the family she worked for. While my grandmother was almost always in a good mood, I remember noting that her enthusiasm was especially pronounced after the guests arrived. My sister and I were in the swings when they pulled up and my grandmother had come to greet them and bring them into the house.

"How you doing, Lucille?" asked Mr. Robert, "Are these your grandchildren?"

"Oh, fair to middlin', Mr. Robert. Yes, suh, they is" Mama Ceal replied loudly and smiling more broadly than the situation seemed to call for. (And was she bowing her head slightly and holding her eyes open a bit wider?)

"Well, I know you must be very proud of them. Della told me they are so smart" added, Ms. Helen.

"Oh, yes ma'am. I am" my grandmother beamed, "But I have to get the switch after them every now and then."

"I imagine you do" laughed Mr. Robert as they walked toward the house.

I remember feeling a bit curious and sad that Mama Ceal seemed a little too fawning and accommodating of the guests. I was also hurt that, while she praised my sister and me for being smart, she also suggested that she spanked us when in fact, I don't recall my grandmother ever spanking us at all. Even as a child, I had figured out that this change in her behavior had something to do with the fact that these people were White. She needed to seem happy and non-threatening. She could be proud, but not too proud. Of course, I would never dare to say anything to her or anyone else about what I saw or how I felt. In addition to not wanting to hurt her feelings, it simply wasn't appropriate for me to question an adult that way or potentially embarrass her. In actuality, I was probably more embarrassed for her than she might have been. I suspect she had long accepted the terms of these rules of engagement as a way of (preserving her) life and didn't see it as any reflection on her so much as on the society that imposed it.

In a similar vein, if she shared my dislike of the nickname the family used for her, I never knew it. Members of the Horton family had explained the nickname's origin at least a couple of times in what they found to be a delightful family story.

"Come on, Carl. You can say it" Eugene Horton coaxed his toddler son. "Lu — cille" he repeated, stretching the word out and exaggerating the pronunciation so that the child could comprehend.

After several attempts, a series of pouty-faced refusals, and the little boy's growing awareness of how much attention he was getting as well as the power he held over his parents, his grandparents, his older sibling and the woman whose name they were trying to get him to say, he replied, "Bobo!"

This unexpected outburst was met with squeals of surprise and laughter, which only prompted him to repeat it. I wonder whether any family members took an unusual enjoyment in the nickname. Would using the nickname "Bobo" remind this woman who seemed to act like part of the family of her place? The nickname was used so much that everyone got accustomed to it, my grandmother included. But were there those who enjoyed the power and privilege of not having to use my grandmother's name and the ability to hang on to a vestige of "a simpler time" when perhaps America was "great"? Over time, "Bobo" became a term of endearment, even if not all of its users were motivated by affection.

I don't know whether my grandmother initially considered the nickname a term of endearment or just an inconsequential — in the whole scheme of things — indignity to endure. It was clear that she loved having a special name within the family that even Carl's and his brother's children sometimes used to refer to her. From my vantage point, I did feel that there were family members who seemed to use the term affectionately but it also caused me a degree of discomfort.

In a strange twist of fate, I sometimes — and occasionally still do — call my son "Bobo" as a shortened version of a nickname I made from his middle name Osei, which morphed from "Oh-see-Bo-see" to "Bo" to occasionally "Bobo." The funny thing is that I didn't even realize the connection or recognize it to be the same word that the Horton family used to refer to my grandmother until relatively recently. Perhaps, in some level of my subconscious mind, I was reappropriating the name to truly be one motivated by love and affection and not possibly tainted by the shadow of white supremacy or racism.

In elementary school, I understood that there was a certain set of rules around using different voices in different situations. While you might get a pass for speaking "proper" with teachers or in class, it was clearly out of place — and sometimes dangerous — to talk the same way on the playground with your friends and classmates. One of the worst condemnations you could receive as a child from your Black friends — and that holds true as an adult — is to be accused of "acting White."

I don't ever remember a "talk" with my parents or other adults about how I should act in front of White people. But somehow, whether it was through observation or the media or the insidious "smog" of racism, I had figured out that adopting the speech and behavior that seemed to be attributed to Whites was at least a pragmatic thing. I'm sure however the lesson was imparted, it was the reason I told myself in grade school that I should have been born White. Not because I thought being White was necessarily better, but because I had dreams of being President one day and Black people don't become President. I look back and grieve for that little boy who came to the "realistic" conclusion that he couldn't be President.

In college, I was aware that I bore the burden of "representing the race" and so I was mindful not to "set us back" (as Wanda Sykes mused in one of her comedy specials) by saying or doing anything to embarrass Black people. No one told me directly that I was the "Black representative" in class, but I was a product of "good home training" so at a minimum I knew what my family expected of me. Even more so, it was communicated effectively enough that I was the resident Black expert through the actions of professors and other students who looked to me and other Black students for the "Black perspective." I never knew whether I could be the model representative, but I was determined not to be the worst and not to reinforce Black stereotypes. As such, I continued to employ the speech and demeanor that seemed best suited for the purpose.

There are plenty of examples of code-switching in popular culture. A 2009 video of President-elect Obama visiting a well-known Black restaurant in Washington, DC, Ben's Chili Bowl, records him using an informal "nah, we straight" when asked if he needed any change after paying for his food. Another 2012 video that went viral captures President Obama meeting the U.S. men's Olympic basketball team and the two distinct ways in which he shook hands with a White assistant coach (the traditional handshake) and a Black NBA player (the "soul" shake that shifts the grip to the thumb followed by an embrace). There is also the sketch of Tyler Perry's character Madea utilizing her best sophistication to greet her church congregation or White people with "Good MornTing."

While both real life and comedic examples illustrate instances in which people use code-switching, they don't give insight into whether the users struggled with conflicting feelings about whether they should have to. To the extent the switching doesn't come easily or feels degrading, who measures or documents the exhaustion generated by maintaining a separate "appropriate" persona in order to be taken seriously, afforded a degree of respect or enjoy a chance at advancement?

As parents seeking to give our children every advantage we could and to help them develop into people who feel confident in themselves and unapologetic about taking up their own space, we were intentional in talking to our kids about our professional lives and sharing lessons we sometimes had to learn through hard knocks and experience. Look adults in the eye when you meet them. Shake their hand firmly to demonstrate your own confidence. Don't hesitate to speak up in a meeting if you have an idea or comment. Look for points of connection and ways to engage in conversation. We wanted them to feel that they had a right to be in whatever environments they found themselves and for people meeting them to immediately see their confidence and strength.

Yet, even as we sought to build these self-possessed, confident people, we also had to engage in the conflicting conduct of having "the talk" with them to ensure they were equipped to navigate situations where their confidence and self-assurance could be a detriment, specifically in situations when they had to deal with the police. We told them both where to keep their hands if they were ever stopped by the police while driving, how to be demonstratively polite and deferential when speaking to them, and how to announce in advance before they moved their hands while engaged with them. There is something profoundly sad and soul-crushing about having to tell your beautiful, amazing child whom you've praised and tried to equip to be strong and independent that those qualities may not be enough to protect them from the systemic racism that exists in our country. It is wearying to worry whether my one hundred twenty pound, 5' 4" daughter, who is dynamo of social activism, defender of the downtrodden and an expressive painter and artist, and my thoughtful 6'3" son, who speaks fluent Italian and rivals trained chefs in the kitchen, could be the next victims of a police officer who only sees them as an "angry Black woman" or "threatening Black man." And so we had the talk and still revisit it periodically in this age of Sandra Bland, George Floyd, and Breonna Taylor. Their lives depend on it.

Unlike my grandmother, who I believe moved in and out of code-switching because it was just accepted as the way things were, I continue to engage in an internal debate as to whether I should even bother paying so much attention to how I speak and present. Does the motivation for code-switching matter anymore? What if it is not an instance in which lives are at stake and instead a matter of a promotion or curating a perception within a social setting? Or what if it is done simply to ensure fair, decent treatment? Does that make it less offensive? Should code-switching still be acceptable as a pragmatic approach to navigating the system or does it amount to inauthenticity that continues to promote the very outdated ways of thinking that spawned it?

What saves me from despair and encourages me that life, systems, and ways of thinking evolve for the better and move forward — perhaps in the steady though sometimes slow way the "arc of the moral universe bends toward justice" — is the attitude of my children and other young people.

Many of their generation rightfully, persistently, defiantly — sometimes forcefully — question me and my generation about the practices we have accepted, promoted and/or failed to dismantle. They have enthusiastically accepted — or wrestled — the baton from those who were the vanguard among previous generations and demanded a world that gives people room to be and express themselves and live exactly as they want. They are leading the way to showcasing the importance of valuing body positivity, celebrating natural hair, rejecting slut-shaming, and supporting genderqueer expression. This mindset finds root in a belief that there is not and should not be a "normal" or standard way of being, which is a good place to start in chipping away at the motivations for code-switching.

And giving Southerners the freedom to say "y'all" and increase the number of syllables in words without concern for judgment is not a bad thing at all.

Lucille and LaRuth in front of Lucille's room

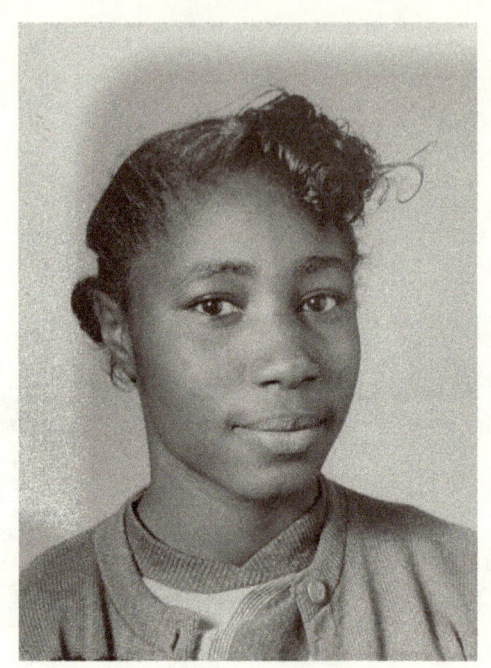

LaRuth in grade school

Above: LaRuth graduating high school

Below: LaRuth in college

Lucille's father, Tommy Hatch

Walter Isodore Eldridge

Elizabeth

Elizabeth and Lucille as young women

Lucille with John and Carl Horton

Walter and Jackie at Tommy's house

Above: LaRuth and Walter, approximately age 4

Below: Jackie and Walter with Lucille

FOURTEEN

"I wish I knew what she was thinking," Lucille pondered to herself as she watched LaRuth fold the clothes that they had brought in from the clothesline. There was so much she wanted to say to her daughter and yet she wasn't sure she knew how. There were so many questions she wanted to ask her daughter and yet she wasn't sure she could stand to hear the answers.

Lucille wondered whether her daughter knew how much she loved her, her only child. She wondered if LaRuth had considered how hard it had been to send her to live with Elizabeth. She turned over and over in her head whether LaRuth had any idea how many times her mother had considered ending the arrangement that they all had deemed "for the best" and instead bringing her home to live in Newcastle. Was it actually true that LaRuth was better off living in Forrest City? Was it? And the one question that she could never voice out loud: Did LaRuth love Elizabeth more than she did her?

"Not today, Satan," she said aloud to herself. It was a beautiful June day and her daughter was with her now. That's what she would focus on. Lucille loved the summers because LaRuth was with her for a couple of months at a time, uninterrupted by the need to return to Forrest City for school. She also sensed, no, she *knew in her heart,* that LaRuth was more relaxed during those extended stays; she seemed to smile more freely and appeared to be less self-conscious than during her weekend visits.

Lucille had loved hearing LaRuth laugh and play with Jesse when they were little, catching a glimpse of her running across an open field with the other children, and seeing the relief in her daughter's eyes when she realized that she wasn't in trouble because she got dirty while playing. But the days of childhood play were behind them and her little girl couldn't be called a "little girl" any longer as middle school was coming to an end and the responsibilities of being a high schooler were imminent.

Lucille could see that even though she was quiet, LaRuth was a pleasant girl, well-mannered, helpful without being asked, and, despite all of Elizabeth's "proper" ways and airs, not fussy to be around. When Lucille needed a hand, LaRuth minded the Horton boys, keeping them occupied outside playing for most of the day when the weather allowed and, when forced inside due to rain, getting them to do a little reading and small art projects without much protest since they liked showing her how "grown up" they were. Occasionally, LaRuth kept her mother company as she did her work in the Hortons' home, sometimes offering to dust or dry dishes or hold the dustpan. It was clear that Elizabeth had seen to it that LaRuth knew how to keep a tidy house.

Lucille could also see that her daughter was becoming a young lady. She recognized that the amount of time they were able to spend together would soon become more and more scarce. As a high school student, LaRuth's schedule was changing and her "free time" was being replaced with the need to begin working and contributing toward her expenses. The split session in school was designed for the very purpose of enabling older students to work — most often in the fields that were a ubiquitous part of the agricultural region in which they lived. Traditionally, ending school in May allowed able-bodied adolescents and teenagers to begin the work of picking beans and chopping cotton, tasks that were required in the late spring and the few weeks leading up to summer. However, sometimes school officials "split" the fall term to allow for breaks spanning parts of September and October when harvesting needs required more bodies and hands.

Lucille used the time she "gained" as a result of shortened summer breaks and fewer weekend visits with LaRuth to take up a number of crafts. Already skilled at sewing because of her grandmother's mentoring, she spent more time making many of her own clothes, including her Sunday dresses for church and more casual shifts that were better than those she could buy in a store. Always a lover of quilting, she collected fabric remnants and swatches from everywhere she could and turned them into beautiful works that years later would be considered folk art but had served as practical necessities for family members, all imbued with her patience, craftsmanship, and love. Not content to stop there, she learned knitting, crocheting, needlepoint, and cross-stitch, the products of which would survive long after her. She enjoyed these crafts, but her prolific handiwork also served to neutralize the void created by the more pronounced loss she felt with less time with LaRuth.

The Horton family also helped fill the vacuum — particularly the children upon whom she doted and into whom she poured her desire to nurture. Like the majority of boys and men of their time, neither Carl nor John Horton were prone to displays of emotion; however, it was clear that they loved "Bobo" and their good-natured mutual teasing, occasional touch of the arm, and offers to help lighten a load were ways they expressed their concern for her well-being. That concern might not rise to the level of fully acknowledging or appreciating the race or class dynamics that governed their relationship, but it was enough that both she and they recognized it as more than polite Southern civility or general regard for the help. Nevertheless, though a few years behind LaRuth, the boys too found new and more exciting diversions that came with their initiation into their teenage years.

As LaRuth, Carl, and John grew older and more independent of her, Lucille continued to devote even more time to her crafts — and to a new pastime.

Letter writing.

FIFTEEN

"I wish I knew what she was thinking," LaRuth thought to herself as she began the trip back to Forrest City after hugging and waving goodbye to her mother.

It truly had been a nice weekend. Yet, despite an enjoyable time and several conversations, LaRuth felt that she and her mother had not really talked — at least not about the things that were important to her. Even though she couldn't imagine life without Liz as her best friend or what it would be like going to the little school near Newcastle, she wondered how her life might be different if she was with her mother all the time. Beyond the what-ifs, questions were LaRuth's frequent companions and she was pestered by the unknown: Did her mother ever wish that they lived together? Did she resent the way Aunt Elizabeth was so quick to introduce LaRuth as *her* daughter? Did her mother miss her?

If she did, she never said.

And LaRuth never asked. Not when she was younger when she might be forgiven a child's impetuousness. She didn't ask even when she became a high schooler, though that status didn't necessarily come with any degree of greater agency. Of course, some of it was the time in which she lived and the fact that she was being raised within a "children are to be seen and not heard" culture. But more of it was due to her own personality and the preternatural sensitivity she possessed as an "old soul." It felt both rude to put her mother on the spot that way and unkind to possibly cause her pain by even asking the questions. Plus, what if the answers weren't what she had hoped they were? She couldn't bring herself to raise any of it, so she came up with her own answers and explanations as to what her mother thought about the situation.

Yes; the weekend was lovely. Earlier that day, she had enjoyed the choir's singing at her mother's church and the extra dose of hugs and well wishes from the Winfreys in addition to having spent time visiting them on Saturday.

Sunday dinner, capped off with Lucille's legendary chocolate pie, had brought the visit to a pleasant but all-too-quick conclusion. She relived it on the late afternoon car ride from Newcastle to Aunt Elizabeth's and Uncle Owen's house.

The visit had started on the prior Friday, which had felt like a good day. For some reason, LaRuth was uncharacteristically excited but she was careful not to be noticeably so. The trip to Newcastle was supposed to start right after school but that was only if the plans held. She had not become a pessimist necessarily; however, now a seasoned teenager, she was skilled in her efforts to keep her expectations low — regarding anything and most anyone — and her hopes moderated. Yet, despite her cultivated cynicism, she had allowed herself to look forward to spending the weekend with her mother, a risk she knew she very well might find herself paying for in despondency and tears.

There had been plenty of weekend trips that somehow had figured out how to let her down for one reason or another. She hated when she had to wait late in the day on Friday for someone to take her to Newcastle and lose those additional hours she could have been with Lucille. She felt even more cheated when she didn't get to go until Saturday morning because she still had to return to Forrest City on Sunday. Worse were the weekends that got canceled altogether because the transportation plan had fallen through, or a conflict had arisen that required LaRuth to stay in Forrest City. Ms. Della moved her regular salon visit to earlier in the week. Uncle Owen had to work through the weekend and couldn't drive her. Or perhaps Aunt Elizabeth had volunteered her for some activity or duty at church. In those instances, the 15 miles to her mother might as well have been a continent away. After enough such experiences, it seemed to LaRuth practical not to allow herself to get disappointed again. But even with the bruises of those letdowns, she couldn't help hoping that this trip came to fruition; it had been a month since she was able to visit her mother.

Thankfully, her ill-advised optimism was rewarded. This trip had started practically perfectly after she and Liz had said their good-byes and promised to reconnect on Monday just before each turned toward her own house on their walk from school. Although she had begun working, Aunt Elizabeth was at home when LaRuth arrived and informed her that her mother and Ms. Della would be there to get her any minute. Aunt Elizabeth urged her to move quickly so that she did not "keep Mrs. Della waiting," with no concern for the fact Lucille was waiting as well. But LaRuth had prepared her bag the night before. Changing quickly out of her school clothes and adding a few items to her case, she was ready to go when the car pulled up to the house following Mrs. Della's hair appointment.

Even though she was eager to be with her mother, LaRuth hoped that she hadn't appeared too anxious to leave as Aunt Elizabeth always seemed a mixture of perturbed and sorrowful when LaRuth left for Newcastle. She couldn't explain her concern but LaRuth felt bad for her aunt's sadness. Perhaps those trips served as a reminder that she was a "mother" in quotation marks and that her "daughter" wasn't hers alone.

The ride to Newcastle felt shorter than usual as Mrs. Della had a ton of questions for LaRuth which seemed to come in rapid succession with barely enough time for her to breathe in between:

"How is school going?"

"What's your favorite subject?"

"Do you like your teachers?"

The questions were punctuated occasionally with Ms. Della's advice.

"Well," Ms. Della continued, "Although I had to practically pull it out of her, your mother tells me you are an excellent student. I'm glad to hear you are enjoying it and doing well. You know that you must study hard and do well in school so that you can make something of yourself. I loved English when I was in school. And loved reading literature. I still do," she added, seemingly lost in her reminiscence.

Otherwise content to let the conversation flow, Lucille was compelled to speak at one point.

"Do you have a boyfriend?" asked Ms. Della.

"No, ma'am," the vigilant mother quickly interjected, "She ain't got no time for a boyfriend. She too busy with her school work."

LaRuth smiled to herself. Both Ms. Della and her mother clearly were in good moods that day — Ms. Della presumably because she was pleased with her hair and the upcoming dinner party she and Lee were to attend on Saturday and her mother perhaps because she was happy to see her she guessed. Whatever the reasons, they were chatting up a storm. LaRuth knew they meant well and the conversation conveyed a genuine concern for her, although it also was clear that they didn't need her participation much for the colloquy to continue. She smiled an even larger smile as she thought this was a real-life example of her new vocabulary word and mentally drafted the obligatory sentence using it: "The two ladies were *loquacious* as they drove down the road."

Once in Newcastle, LaRuth put her things in Lucille's room and then walked to join her mother in the Hortons' kitchen. Evidently her mother had done much of the dinner preparation before she and Ms. Della had left for the hairdresser. LaRuth could smell the hint of garlic and onion in the green beans that were simmering on the stove. She moved to the kitchen table to cream the potatoes that had been diced and seasoned and were waiting in a large ceramic bowl that sat next to a masher, one that was metal and round with holes in it, an obvious upgrade from the wooden one LaRuth had once remembered seeing there. Her mother was already frying chicken and an uncut pound cake winked from a cake plate covered by a glass dome.

"Thank you, baby," Lucille said to her daughter as she started mashing the potatoes. LaRuth wondered why the Hortons preferred the phrase "creamed" potatoes as opposed to "mashed" like most folks said.

"Tomorrow, I want you to go by and spend a little time with Effie before you go to see the Winfreys, okay?" The questioning intonation was just politeness since LaRuth knew that her mother's wish was not dependent on whether she agreed.

"Yes ma'am," LaRuth replied.

"How is Dene?" asked her mother. "Are y'all still in the same classes together?"

"She's fine," answered LaRuth. "We have a lot of our classes together but not all of them."

"That's good. I ain't seen Cousin Lizzie in a month of Sundays. I'll have to write her a letter. I know yo' best friend is that little Lucas girl, and I'm glad y'all is such good friends but you make sho' Dene know you always her family."

"Yes, ma'am," LaRuth answered. "I believe she knows that, Mama. We have a bunch of the same friends, so we are around each other a lot. Aunt Elizabeth let me spend the night with her two Fridays ago. Aunt Lizzie is doing good, too."

The banter flowed easily as they finished the meal. Lucille updated LaRuth on the health of the family that Lucille had seen lately; the new dress pattern she had bought; and the latest happenings at her little church they were to attend on Sunday.

Once everything was dished up and the Hortons were having their dinner in the dining room, LaRuth and Lucille sat down at the kitchen table to eat the chicken, beans and creamed potatoes that Lucille had set aside for them. They didn't talk much then, mindful of not being loud or distracting to Mr. Lee and Ms. Della.

After dinner, still in their respective spaces, they all had dessert of the pound cake and the store-bought vanilla ice cream that never tasted quite as good as the homemade version Lucille made.

"Lucille!" yelled Lee from the dining room, and over the chiding of his wife.

"Yes, suh," Lucille replied, getting up from the table to go to the dining room.

"Don't get up," he continued yelling, "This cake sure is good. You outdid yo'self."

"Thank you, Mr. Lee," she responded, sitting back down to smile at LaRuth and finish her dessert.

After the dining room was cleared and the kitchen cleaned, the Hortons invited Lucille and LaRuth to sit with them for some television.

LaRuth didn't mind watching television with the Hortons but it was never entirely relaxing as she was keen not to embarrass her mother. Not because of her mother's expressed concerns but because she could hear Aunt Elizabeth's voice in her head, admonishing her to be mindful of her posture, to not laugh too loudly, to remember that she was a young lady. After the week's episodes of *Kukla, Fran and Ollie*, *The Adventures of Rin Tin Tin*, and *Blondie*, Lucille made sure the Hortons didn't need anything else before she left their house for the evening.

Back in her room, Lucille turned on the radio for LaRuth so that she could listen to *Amos 'n' Andy*, and Bing Crosby's show while Lucille laid out the pattern pieces on the fabric she planned to use for the new dress. She had pressed out the wrinkles in the tissue of the patterns and was ready to pin the pieces to the fabric and cut after laying everything on the cutting board.

When it was time for bed, LaRuth realized it had been a pretty uneventful evening, but she felt a calm and peacefulness that she needed and could sense that a restful sleep was ahead.

SIXTEEN

The next day, after a breakfast of Cream of Wheat with sliced bananas and a little brown sugar, a slice of toast, and coffee — which was more milk and sugar than actual coffee — LaRuth left her mother in the middle of preparations for the Hortons' Sunday dinner and walked the 20 minutes to her grandmother Effie's house. It was a little farther than the Winfreys' home, but she was happy to save them for last since she was most excited to see them and she didn't expect her time with her grandmother to be especially long. Plus, LaRuth didn't want to say to her grandmother that she had stopped to see the Winfreys before coming to see her if asked.

Knocking on the screen door and yelling in "Hello, Grandmother. It's LaRuth," she found Effie in her little kitchen snapping beans. After a perfunctory hug of putting her arms around her grandmother's shoulders and Effie raising one hand to pat her granddaughter's arm, LaRuth pulled a chair up to the table and joined the work.

Not a tall woman, sitting there, Effie seemed even smaller than LaRuth remembered. Just over five feet, Effie was slender but sturdy and determined enough that it would take more than a strong gust of wind to knock her over. LaRuth could see the age in the dark brown skin of her grandmother's face, a face that was weathered though not filled with an excessive number of wrinkles. Her head was covered by an understated headscarf that was entirely utilitarian but not unattractive.

The chill that lingered in the air of this early spring day accounted for the layers of clothing Effie was wearing — which didn't seem to follow a particular rhyme or reason for being worn together other than to provide warmth — along with the small fire that was ablaze in the cast iron potbelly stove. Above the slightly musty, stale aroma that signaled this was a house of someone old with ancient thoughts, wounds, and regrets, LaRuth could smell the smoke from the squat, coal-black stove. She suspected that the Winfreys must have brought wood for her grandmother since she was not likely to still be using an ax. The smell of burning wood would occasionally remind LaRuth of Effie long after her grandmother had passed and after LaRuth had become a grandmother herself.

"I didn't know you was coming," Effie said looking up from the beans in her bowl while still breaking the tips off the ends. "You sho' done growed a heap since I seen you."

"Yes, ma'am," LaRuth replied. "This is my first time in a while."

"How is school? Is you gettin' yo' lessons good?" she questioned.

"Yes, ma'am. I'm trying. My last grade report was pretty good."

"That's good," Effie replied. "Although I hear tell them grades is more than pretty good. I know 'Cille is proud," she added as she reached across the table to pat LaRuth's hand. LaRuth noted that her grandmother's hands were a bit calloused but that didn't detract from the warmth and love she felt at their touch. With both feeling a little awkward and not knowing what to do, Effie quickly withdrew her hand and asked, "How is she?"

"She's good," LaRuth answered, continuing to snap. "She said to tell you hello and that she will see you at church tomorrow."

"Mmm hmm," her grandmother uttered. Ending the exchange for a few minutes.

LaRuth liked her grandmother well enough although she wasn't especially close to her. She hadn't spent as much time with her lately as she had when she was younger and her mother would send her to spend the night. For whatever reason, they never forged an intimate connection. But LaRuth knew that they liked each other. Her grandmother didn't hug her tight or make a big fuss the way the Winfreys did whenever she saw them, but Effie would make tea cakes or have something sweet when she knew LaRuth was coming. She'd try to have at least a couple of quarters to give her as a small gesture. They shared what might be called a kind of tenderness, a genuine, if muted, affection.

"Yo mama is a good woman, LaRuth," Effie said, resuming the dormant conversation. "You know that?"

"Yes, ma'am," LaRuth answered.

"You might know some but you don't know it all," Effie replied.

Drawing in a deep breath, Effie continued, "Before your father drowned, I wasn't real nice to yo' mama. For a long time." After an extended pause, Effie began speaking again: "But she always checked on me after she moved out. She still let you come see 'bout me and spend time with me. She still sends me a mess o' greens, or some cake, or a plate o' food every now and then."

Almost sighing to herself, she finished, "I ain't never told her how much I 'ppreciated that. But I'm telling you. She a good woman."

"Yes, ma'am" was all LaRuth knew to respond.

Later, when she returned after her visits, fingering the coins Effie had pressed into her hand as she said goodbye, LaRuth started to tell her mother what her grandmother had said about her. But the time didn't seem right. Plus, how was she supposed to bring it up anyway? Just blurt it out? The more she turned it over and over in her head, the more she realized she didn't want to make her mother sad by saying anything about her father. Somewhere along the way, something had convinced her that she shouldn't talk about him. So she let it go. She did tell her mother that Effie had given her two quarters as she wrapped them in her handkerchief and put them into her bag. Thanks to her grandmother, LaRuth could treat herself and Liz to a movie or maybe a coke float and fries the next time they were allowed to go to the hamburger joint.

It had been a lovely day.

SEVENTEEN

Lucille had learned that it hurt less if she didn't watch the car disappear out of sight when LaRuth left to return to Forrest City. After a hug goodbye and a quick look to make sure she didn't miss her daughter's last wave so that she could return the gesture, Lucille gathered herself to go back to the Hortons' to finish a couple of final Sunday tasks and see if they needed anything before going to her room.

Dinner had ended a while ago, but there were enough leftovers in case anyone needed a snack before bedtime. On this particular Sunday, Lee and Della Horton were joined in their den by their son Eugene, his wife Marian, and their grandsons John and Carl, not unusual since their house was less than a hundred feet away. The family was watching television and having seconds of the coconut cake that had been dessert. After declining to join them and ensuring there was nothing more she needed to do, Lucille washed and dried the cake plate and left for her room with the last slice of cake that she had wrapped in a piece of wax paper. She too would enjoy another piece of her successful attempt at trying a new recipe.

Back in her room, she turned on the Memphis radio station that played gospel on Sunday evenings — a soloist was beginning the first verse of *Precious Lord, Take My Hand* — and resumed piecing the quilt she had started the week before.

"Her" room actually wasn't *hers* since she didn't own it. But it was hers in the sense that it represented a space that she alone occupied and controlled for all practical purposes. It was her bedroom, living room, and craft room. It also served as her prayer closet, her retreat from the demands of housekeeping and child minding, her sanctuary for private reflection — all in an area that was smaller than the room where the Hortons were watching their Sunday evening shows. Without the least bit of envy, though fully aware of the differences between her room and the multiple, large rooms in the Hortons' home, Lucille was genuinely grateful for the compact, contained space she called hers. It was just enough, and she could do all that she needed in it. Admittedly, it was more structurally sound than the house she had shared with Walter and Effie. The floorboards didn't creak every time she walked across them. Even better, she didn't worry about the smell of smoke from a potbelly stove or the annoyance of pests creeping into the various crevices. Except for the rare instance of a necessary repair, no one other than she and LaRuth or other family members whom she invited came into the space.

The fan pattern on the quilt she was working on was simple but it required a lot of attention as she operated her foot-pedal sewing machine. She welcomed the tediousness of the work as she stitched the pieces of cloth together to make the individual squares that she ultimately brought together to make the quilt. She had seen some truly elaborate versions of this quilt with carefully coordinated and complementary fabric choices repeated neatly over and over such that each square was a mirror copy of the next and the finished product looked store bought. Those were for sure beautiful quilts, but she had chosen a different approach for this one that she was making for herself — or maybe for LaRuth if she might want it.

The fabrics that Lucille had selected were a combination of random pieces that she had left over from various sewing projects — a dress or curtains she had made, remnants she collected from other ladies at church who didn't quilt and who had no use for them, as well as material that she had purchased on trips to Forrest City with Ms. Della. To most people, the assortment represented a jumble of mix-matched odds and ends that could not have much purpose. But Lucille loved taking the random textures and patterns and putting them together to create something useful — and beautiful.

As she sewed, Lucille started humming along with the singer on the radio, the words floating through her consciousness: *Precious Lord, take my hand. Lead me on, let me stand.*

What looked like a confusion of cloth scraps and colors and patterns reminded Lucille of how confused and disordered her life felt sometimes. While she believed herself generally to be safe with the Hortons, she was still a Negro woman in a society that placed little value on her life and among many White people who held an abiding dislike if not hatred for anyone who looked like her. It was not uncommon to hear of someone having been harassed or attacked for no apparent reason other than they were Black. Everyone knew of Negroes who had the misfortune of crossing paths with some White character who felt like taking out whatever angst that plagued them that day on the first person legally and socially unable to defend themselves without consequence. Dessie Mae had told her about her neighbors' son who was almost beaten in front of the drug store downtown because a White man believed that the boy had bumped into him intentionally. And the daughter of one of the ushers on her usher board had been followed by a group of White boys from another county until a car drove up and the boys turned around.

But that was just the way things were, that was the regular disorder, threat, and anxiety that Black folks faced.

I am tired. I am weak. I am worn. Through the storm, through the night . . .

As she sewed, Lucille slowly realized— as she experienced occasionally — that she was feeling especially low and lonely. She considered but dismissed the idea that it was just the words of the song that had her feeling this way. Had they sung that at Walter's funeral? She couldn't remember. She was finding the music both depressing and comforting at the same time.

Although missing Walter and LaRuth, Lucille knew not to question God's ways. At least, tonight, she was resolute in her belief that LaRuth needed to be in Forrest City at that school if she was going to have a real chance at having a decent life. But LaRuth's absence magnified the loss of Walter — and Lucille's loneliness. Despite her fortitude and determination to try to be content, there were days when she couldn't help wondering why she wasn't living the life she and Walter had planned.

Walter had dreamt of buying a few acres of land. They could plant some cotton since the gin was right there near them. He felt Mr. Horton was a decent man as far as White folks go and they could get a reasonable if not fair price for the cotton he grew. He also wanted to have space for a garden to grow their own food and to be able to sell some of the produce to bring in more money. Eventually, Lucille would give up doing laundry and focus on their own home and family.

As she continued working on the quilt, she wrinkled her brow. Although she could not remember them talking about it, she was sure Walter would have wanted to have at least one more baby, maybe two — if they could. It had taken them a while to have LaRuth. In her mind, she had already named their son Lil' Walter. Not that she planned to let anyone call him that even if they did name a boy Walter, but it had been her own private joke. She envisioned LaRuth as a very protective big sister and "little Mama" to her brother — or sister if that was how the Lord chose to bless them. Imagining all of the wonderful matching clothes she could have sewn for them made the corners of her mouth turn up ever so slightly as her eyes simultaneously welled with tears that never fell.

When my way grows drear, Precious Lord, linger near.

Usually, she could keep at bay the deep ache and longing she felt for Walter — both the earnest boy who wasn't like the other boys in her grandparents' church and the man who had won her heart and fathered her child. But this day, sitting there thinking about seeing LaRuth leave brought back the emptiness that she couldn't fill with her busyness or the gospel quartet singing on the radio or a moist slice of cake. Even as she tried to focus on the quilt and the music playing on the radio, she couldn't dismiss the lingering thoughts that she was now over 40 years old, living alone, and the widow of a good man whom she had given her love to and who, inexplicably, didn't come home alive from a night out with his friends the way he had done on many times before.

She knew they had been drinking, but no one believed that the men were drunk. Leon had said as much. But that hadn't stopped some of the gossipmongers from whispering the possibility, even though none of the men — and certainly not Walter — had that kind of reputation. But it was hard to hold on to that knowledge with the certainty she once had now that he had been gone for so many years now. Lord knows it was hard not to be angry — at whom she wasn't sure since she couldn't let herself be angry at God and wouldn't let herself be angry at Walter — that he hadn't on his own or that she hadn't suggested that he just stay home that night.

Hear my cry, hear my call. Hold my hand, lest I fall.

The needle she was using to finish by hand a small portion of one of the squares pricked her finger. She barely noticed it. In addition to being lost in her thoughts, her fingers had become calloused, an adaptation to protect her from the inevitable future pains that were to come with the more time she spent quilting, crafting beauty out of chaos. Perhaps in time, her heart might do the same or take on some other form of evolution that might make her losses and sorrows easier to bear. For now, for tonight, the load of those woes seemed pretty heavy indeed. Still, the painless jab pulled her back to the work before her.

Lead me on to the light. Take my hand, Precious Lord, and lead me home.

Even as she continued to indulge her moments of melancholy, she couldn't help being pleased with how the quilt squares were coming along.

Yes, ma'am. This was going to be one of her best quilts yet.

EIGHTEEN

"Girl, you crazy. I still can't believe you did that," LaRuth said to Liz as they exchanged their morning textbooks for the afternoon ones in their lockers.

"I told you I was gonna do it," Liz replied with a chuckle.

"But I didn't think you were serious. And I definitely didn't think I would win."

"Girl," Liz continued, "I knew you was gonna win. People like you. Besides, I been bettin' on you for a long time — even when you weren't bettin' on yo-self."

LaRuth smiled that her best friend looked quite pleased with herself. Liz was right that LaRuth would never have expressed an interest in being a class officer to her classmates, let alone submit her name. But Liz was even more convinced that LaRuth could be elected than she had let on.

Truth be told, despite being a bit overwhelmed, LaRuth was pleased too. It was enough that Liz had nominated her, considering that Liz's own sister was running for the position as well. That her classmates had elected her senior class secretary was even harder to take in. Part of the reason LaRuth was in a state of disbelief is that she couldn't understand how it had happened. She certainly wasn't one of the most stylish girls at school as Aunt Elizabeth had seen to that. Her clothes were sensible and tasteful but on the cutting edge of fashion they were not. Elizabeth preferred simple pieces in muted colors. Occasionally, LaRuth was allowed to use some of the money she made to buy an outfit or piece that she liked but she was no fashion plate. Content to stay in the background, she also wasn't one of the "popular" girls who went to all of the parties or sought a lot of attention. While LaRuth had a good sense that she got along with pretty much everyone, she didn't think that might result in anything like this. By contrast, Liz was sure that the fact that LaRuth was nice, unassuming, and hadn't felt like she was supposed to win were the reasons the other seniors chose her for the leadership role. Whatever her classmates' motivations,

LaRuth's election was both a surprise and an honor to her. The added bonus was that Aunt Elizabeth was very pleased.

Of course, her mother would be excited as well, but she was proud of anything LaRuth did as long as she was kind to others and tried to do her best. And although Lucille never encouraged her to be disobedient, LaRuth got the sense that her mother wasn't terribly upset on the rare occasions when, as she got older, she spoke up for herself to challenge some of Aunt Elizabeth's rules or press a point if it really mattered to her.

Aunt Elizabeth, on the other hand, had higher expectations than a kindly disposition. It was clear to LaRuth that Aunt Elizabeth wanted — no needed — LaRuth to be practically perfect. Elizabeth was singularly focused on raising LaRuth as an example of a well-mannered young Negro woman. This goal was not just for folks in her family and the people in her community. After all, White folks were always watching.

"LaRuth, did I tell you what Dr. O'Connor said to me the other day?" Elizabeth asked as she stirred the pot of beans that was just about finished on the stove.

"No, ma'am," LaRuth responded in the middle of folding towels at the kitchen table. "Who is Dr. O'Connor?"

"He is one of the doctors I work with at the hospital. He asked me how you were doing in school, and I told him you were doing well and keeping your grades up so that you can go to college. He said 'Is that right?' and that he always knew you were a smart girl based on how I had talked about you. He said you gon' be a fine young lady someday."

"Yes, ma'am," LaRuth replied, not knowing exactly how she was supposed to respond to that piece of information.

It didn't seem to matter at that point since Elizabeth had moved on to tasting the pot liquor from the beans and appeared lost in the moment of the memory with Dr. O'Connor.

By no means was Elizabeth alone in her mission to demonstrate that she and her family should be considered exemplars of their race. It is not unusual for those in a minority group trying to establish their place in a majority culture to seek to demonstrate their value by upholding the mores championed by that majority culture. At a minimum, people who ascribed to this school of thought were intent on not confirming the stereotypes that were associated with those who looked like them. Hence, like many Black people then and now, Elizabeth wanted to distance herself and LaRuth from any behavior that might show them to be, among other things, simple-minded, loud, lazy, uncouth, "loose" or immoral. However, Elizabeth expected LaRuth to go beyond undercutting stereotypes: she wanted her to be one of those who helped "lift" the race.

In addition to placing these expectations upon LaRuth, Elizabeth did her own small part to lift the race. She trained to be a nurse's assistant at the hospital, which she believed afforded her a certain level of respectability and status above women who cleaned other people's houses. Yet, she felt her greatest achievement would be realizing her goal of raising an accomplished daughter and thereby showing that she was a good mother. She didn't go so far as to *tell* people that she was a good mother, but she could certainly share the successes of her daughter — at work, at church, and in the neighborhood. Given their family's lack of education and prominence, Elizabeth didn't necessarily dream of LaRuth being among the group of doctors, ministers, lawyers, or business owners who were considered "high-society" Negroes; however, she could make sure her daughter was considered respectable by any measure.

Elizabeth was very pleased with herself as she could see that her work was paying off. In addition to having good grades, LaRuth's quiet, polite demeanor was often read as mannerly and polished by a certain set of Negro women who placed a huge emphasis on civility and respectability. With similar outlooks as Elizabeth, these women hoped that their examples countered the images of uneducated and less refined Negroes. Through cultivating the finer qualities of womanhood, they were contributing to the advancement of their race by showing that Black families were as capable as White ones of making contributions to society at large. Through their demonstrated "respectability" they showed the White world that they deserved to be treated with fairness and respect.

It was most likely the way that LaRuth carried herself, with Elizabeth's voice ever present in her ear, that led to her being invited to become a member of Junior Semper Fidelis. The "junior" group was an adult-sponsored teen version of the adult women's Semper Fidelis club. Similar to social clubs for White women, Semper Fidelis members held meetings, advanced civic projects, and promoted mutual aid within the Black community, which included helping the less fortunate. Additionally, the ladies played bridge and encouraged etiquette and genteel behavior befitting respectable, upstanding Negro ladies. With their teen counterparts, club members enjoyed teas, recitals, field trips, and other social gatherings and activities. Some of LaRuth's teachers who were members had nominated her. Elizabeth was thrilled when LaRuth brought home the printed invitation to become a member. Notwithstanding the fact that she neither was nor expected to be invited to the adult club, Elizabeth felt validated.

One afternoon as she hung up her coat in the entry area of the school library where the month's meeting was being held, LaRuth was greeted by school counselor and club member Juanita Agnes.

"LaRuth," she observed, "That's a very smart blouse you're wearing."

"Thank you, Mrs. Agnes," she answered.

LaRuth wasn't responding simply out of courtesy. The contrasting stitching on the Peter Pan collar of the pale blue blouse she had on that day and the long, mid-calf hunter green pencil skirt was an outfit that she had selected on one of her few shopping trips without Aunt Elizabeth.

"You're welcome. Now don't forget that you need to have your recitation memorized next week so that we are ready for the Spring Social at the end of the month"

"Yes, ma'am," LaRuth responded.

"I suspect you will be hearing about college any day now," she added.

"Yes, ma'am," LaRuth replied again. "I hope it is soon."

"Be sure to tell your aunt I asked about her. Go ahead and join the other girls finishing up the posters for the dance."

"Yes, ma'am."

LaRuth thought the club was interesting enough but she could have been just as happy had she not been asked to join. She leaned more to the mindset of others in her family who, unlike Elizabeth, held little interest in or concern about women's social clubs — Negro ones or otherwise. To her cousin Dene and Aunt Dessie, those ladies seemed stuck up and pretentious. They held no delusions that White folks were going to treat any of them better because they were educated, laughed politely or knew how to eat little sandwiches at tea. By contrast, Lucille always found LaRuth's club updates interesting since she had her own experience assisting Ms. Della with her entertaining duties. LaRuth also got a chance to observe some of the finer points of entertaining on weekends when her mother was helping prepare for a sorority meeting or dinner party, so she was comfortable navigating the club's etiquette and hosting lessons.

On another occasion, LaRuth found herself the object of praise from the club president.

"That is an excellent table setting, LaRuth," commented Clovis Moody, wife of a prominent local minister and who also happened to be hosting the meeting at her home. "You have every single piece in its correct place. You will make an excellent hostess when your time comes."

"Thank you," LaRuth answered, recognizing that she had helped her mother set a formal table countless times before.

LaRuth had no plans or desire to be one of the grande dames that the Semper Fidelis members seemed to hold up as their exemplar. However, that the club helped keep Aunt Elizabeth happy was more than worth the time and attention it required. Besides, some of the girls were actually nice, and she enjoyed many of the activities that the club sponsored. Society matron or not, she liked having access to the information that was shared — especially about college — and getting a chance to compare what she had seen at the Hortons' with how the Negro elite conducted themselves.

Now on the verge of graduating from high school, LaRuth could not have imagined her life when she first came to live with her Aunt Elizabeth and Uncle Owen. While part of her still wished that she could have been with her mother, she also recognized that she had enjoyed her school experience in Forrest City and she knew that it was certainly better than the experience would have been had she gone to school in the country. Sure, Aunt Elizabeth had been very strict, but there had been a lot of other positives as well. Aunt Elizabeth had mellowed — if only a bit — over the years and Uncle Owen was a nice buffer even if it was mostly behind the scenes. She couldn't have asked for a better friend than Liz. The periodic visits to Aunt Dessie's house were a welcome respite from Aunt Elizabeth's strictness. She got to see her cousin Dene often and had several other friends. She had also been allowed to get a small after-school job babysitting. Aunt Elizabeth was even letting her pick her own prom dress — within certain parameters of course.

Although LaRuth could appreciate why being in Forrest City had been good, the ache for her mother never fully left her even while it became less pronounced. As much as she trusted and otherwise confided in Liz, this particular sentiment she kept to herself, voicing it only within the walls of her mind. She couldn't suppress the "what-ifs" of how their relationship might have been different if they had lived together instead of connecting during weekend visits, and summer and holiday breaks. She never questioned her mother's love for her but surely, her mother had to see and feel the awkwardness and distance between them. What if her mother loved her as a mother is supposed to do but simply *didn't like her* very much?

For her part, Lucille knew that LaRuth's absence was a self-inflicted injury, one for which there was no complete balm. She reminded herself constantly that sending her daughter away was for the best, even if it meant that they might not be as close as Lucille otherwise wanted them to be. What if LaRuth preferred Elizabeth as her mother, and actually loved her *more*? To talk to LaRuth about the invisible but palpable fence that kept them from genuine emotional intimacy felt like pouring salt in the wound. She found it frustrating that she could never be sure what LaRuth was feeling and found it safer to enjoy what they had than to ask her and risk damaging it. Perhaps it was safer not to know and let things continue as they were.

Whether reluctance to be vulnerable, fear of hurt, lack of courage, or avoidance of conflict, neither Lucille nor LaRuth found the nerve to raise the uncomfortable issue that plagued them both. A conversation between the two about how the separation had impacted them never occurred. Any mutual recognition of their shared pain and trauma would forever be lost to time.

NINETEEN

Route 1 Box 315
Forrest City Ark

Dear Walter & Girl Friend
Oh I were scared I would
spell her name Wright
So I just say Girl Friend
I realy were glad to see
her and like her very
much. just sorry I don't
have any Cake to serve
you all But I ask your
Mother what day you
all would be comen so
I could have made a
Cake But it were glad to
see all I you all every
one like the Girl Friend
you all be good and
studdy heard Hi to all
I love you
Momma C.

> Route 1 Box 315
> Forrest City, Ark
>
> Dear Walter & Girlfriend
> Oh I were sceard I wound spell her name wright so I just say Girlfriend. I really were glad to see her and like her very much. Just sorry I dent have any cake to serve you all but I ask your mother what day you all would be comen so I could have made a cake but it were good to see all of you all. Everyone like the Girl Friend. You all be good and studdy heard. Hi to all.
> I love you
> Moma C.

Mama Ceal didn't have a lot of what most people consider valuable material possessions to leave us when she died. Of course, there were treasured family pictures that captured both noteworthy and uneventful moments in time and those that gave face to names of family members who died before we had the chance to meet them. I'm reminded of the one picture of her husband, my grandfather, Walter Isadore Eldridge, after whom I am named. In the picture, he is wearing an earnest expression that is difficult to read. While I'm also familiar with the phenomenon of people not smiling in old pictures, this expression is not simply one in which he is choosing not to smile. There is more to it, a force and an urgency that is just out of reach of understanding. Is he agitated? Frustrated? Focused on some plan he has for his life, for his wife and family? Whatever occupied his thoughts in that picture was lost to me long before I was born since his life was cut short at 33. Leaving my grandmother with only 13 years of marriage; leaving my mother with just over six years of sharing the planet and fewer actual memories of him; and leaving me — or perhaps the hope of me — with his name and a picture that appreciates in emotional value the older I get.

Fortunately, one of my grandmother's great pastimes was quilting and needlework, including embroidery, knitting, crocheting, and cross stitch. As a result, we have wall hangings, needlework crafts, and numerous quilts that she made. Some of the quilts are traditional ones that she pieced from fabric scraps and from fabrics that she purchased. Some are large, cross-stitched panels that were sewn together and then quilted. There are quilts with red birds, ones with simple star patterns and others with elaborate flower appliques, ones with Dutch girls, and ones with overlapping circles known as the "Wedding Ring" pattern. Juliette and I have one that my mother gave us that is a cross-stitched ribbon that ties in a bow at the top of the quilt in green and blue thread. Originally, it was an anniversary present to my parents. Among several others, we also have one that she made after the birth of our daughter that is a simple fan pattern but made — at Juliette's and my request — entirely in red, black, and green, the colors of the Pan African flag: red standing for the blood shed by Africans and their descendants, black standing for Black people, and green standing for Africa. (The flag was adopted by Marcus Garvey's Universal Negro Improvement Association in 1920 and designed to serve as a rallying symbol to represent people of the African Diaspora.)

In addition to her quilts, we also have numerous recipes (and the memories) of dishes she made for us. She found recipes in the Southern Living magazines that Mrs. Della subscribed to, in the local daily and weekly newspapers that came to the house, and in random magazines sitting in the waiting rooms of doctors' offices. Some of them were quite simple like making breadsticks from hot dog buns. Others required more involved steps to produce a multi-layered ravioli or sumptuous cake. Her recipe for the chocolate coconut ball candy (think bite-sized Mounds nuggets) has become a Christmas tradition for our family — we have made it every Christmas for over 20 years — and been introduced to hundreds of our extended family and friends.

One year, Juliette and other family members were out running last minute errands and the job of mixing the candy ingredients was assigned to me. The recipe does not call for a lot of liquid so the task of blending all the ingredients requires some effort. It must be done by hand per Mama Ceal's instruction. At one point, I was convinced that someone must have copied the recipe incorrectly because it seemed to be getting more and more difficult to get all of the dry ingredients as moist and blended as I knew they were supposed to be. When I stopped to stretch my hands and considered how hard it was to make this candy, I thought about Mama Ceal doing this at a much older age than I was at the time, with hands that had become arthritic because she had picked and chopped untold pounds of cotton, washed tons of clothes on washboards and in lye soap, and swept and mopped miles of floors long before I was born. I thought about how much harder it had to be for her, how much more it must have hurt her hands to do this mixing and my eyes filled with tears at the realization of the devotion she showed and the pain she endured just to make that candy for us. Being able to touch physical items that she touched, making candy in the same way that she did have a comforting and grounding quality for me. Looking at pictures that she saved and that captured her image bridge the divide created by death. The rituals of shared activity, the tangible products of her handiwork, they all bring forth emanations that make her spirit and influence alive and relevant even in the absence of her physical presence.

But I realize that there are also inheritances we hold that she probably had not intended to leave us. There are pains and hurts and traumas that have traveled and survived generations to impact and influence how I make my way in this world, how I interact with my family, my friends, my colleagues.

I have no doubt in my mind that my mother and Mama Ceal loved each other deeply. Yet, as much as they loved each other, there was also an awkwardness, a distance between them. I believe that uncomfortable space was rooted in their respective hurts, ones that find origin in the decision to send my mother to live with her Aunt Elizabeth, Mama Ceal's sister-cousin, the woman who was like another grandmother to me and whom my sister and I call Momo.

Mama Ceal and my grandfather Walter lived in Newcastle, a very rural part of St. Francis County, Arkansas. Because the school that my mother otherwise would have attended was small and lacked the resources of both the White school in the area and the Black school roughly 10 miles away in the next largest town of Forrest City, my grandparents made the difficult decision to send her to live in Forrest City. Forrest City is named after Nathan Bedford Forrest, Confederate Army general and first Grand Wizard of the Ku Klux Klan. It is ironic that the town that was the namesake of one who sought to deny opportunity to Black people is where my grandparents sent my mother so that she could go to a better school and, hopefully, have the opportunity to do more than the agricultural or domestic work that most likely awaited her completion of school in "the country." In addition to the obvious fact that my mother could not be with her parents every day, the decision was even more difficult because she was their only child and had come several years after they were married and presumably tried to have children. Although they made this sacrifice to do what was best for my mother, it came with many unanticipated consequences.

Not because she was ungrateful but because she was just a child when she was first sent away, my mother wanted to be with her own mother and father. It was hard for my mother not to feel given away, if not abandoned. And living with Aunt Elizabeth was not easy. She was a strict disciplinarian and insisted that everything be neat and tidy, not necessarily the most welcoming of environments for a little girl. There wasn't a lot of room for outside playtime and Aunt Elizabeth didn't have a very nurturing personality.

This is not to suggest that Aunt Elizabeth didn't love my mother for I think we all, Mama Ceal included, believe that she absolutely did. However, Aunt Elizabeth loved her the best way that she knew how — even if it wasn't quite the way that my mother needed. She was proud to be raising my mother and consistently referred to her as "my daughter," a practice she continued for the rest of her life. Fortunately for my mother, she had Aunt Elizabeth's husband, Uncle Owen, also after whom I am named and whom my sister and I called "Papa." He and my mother became buddies. Truly a man of few words, he brought her little treats of candy, the existence of which they kept to themselves, shared conspiratorial but harmless winks to lighten the atmosphere when needed, and planned rare but occasional excursions.

At least early on, the stark difference between life in "the city" and life in "the country" is why the weekends my mother was able to go visit her parents were pure joy for her. Running outside, playing cards, being allowed to get dirty, all made for a more relaxed, more fun and less tense existence. Those weekends and the relationship with Uncle Owen made my mother's time in Forrest City bearable. After the death of her father, and as she got older and had more of her friends in the city, the weekend trips grew fewer, more sporadic. Although she never told her mother that she would rather be with her, she never quite got over her feeling of being somewhat disconnected.

From Mama Ceal's perspective, she wanted my mother with her as much as my mother wanted to be with her. However, she knew that having the chance to go to the city school had to be better for my mother. Yet, she had also convinced herself that her little one room attached to a barn that lacked hot water and the neat, uncluttered order of Elizabeth's house couldn't possibly be what my mother preferred after living in the city. On top of it all, she was often present to hear Elizabeth call LaRuth her daughter and I suspect that never ceased to prick my grandmother's heart. If it meant — whether actually true or not — that her daughter loved another woman more than her and preferred to be in that woman's company, then that was the price she had to pay to ensure the better life she wanted for her child. Not until late in life did Mama Ceal even breathe a hint of the hurt she felt about the time she missed with my mother and then only to my sister and me. In those instances, she didn't express outright how allowing Momo to raise my mother and hearing Momo claim my mother as her daughter impacted her. Instead, she made occasional snide comments about how "stuck up" Momo could be or imitated Momo's pretentiousness with a pinched expression. While sometimes funny to witness, we also came to understand that that was the way she was able to give voice to the wounds she carried because of her separation from her daughter.

I don't know why my mother and my grandmother never talked to each other to say how they really felt but their awkwardness with each other also created an awkwardness between my mother and her children. She was absolutely loving and supportive of us. I never ever doubted that my mother loved me. But being demonstratively affectionate my mother was not, as if it were a luxury she had long ago determined she couldn't afford. Of course, we always hugged and kissed when we visited each other or said goodbye, but we never had moments where we snuggled together on the couch to watch a movie or stood embracing just because we were near each other.

Even as an adult I took special notice of moments of physical affection with my mother because it was so rare. By way of example, in one of my sporadic periods of trying to keep a journal, I recorded a moment that stood out for me when my mother visited me for the Easter holiday during law school. It was 1989 and I was 24 years old. It was the Saturday of her several-day visit and she, Juliette, and I were walking the National Mall. We were near the Capitol building and Juliette offered to get the car so that we could leisurely walk in the direction of the Lincoln Monument. As we walked, my mother and I talked and at some point, I took her hand. I remember feeling odd that I did that but she didn't draw away and we walked holding hands for quite a while. It was significant enough and uncharacteristic enough that I made a mental note of both the moment and the happiness it gave me to have that experience.

I think it took the birth of my children and their unbridled affection to give my mother the permission and freedom to be more affectionate. I love watching them grab her for a spontaneous hug or nestle in next to her if they are sitting talking or watching TV. I am certain that my children don't have the sense of my mother not being affectionate in the same way that I do. Similarly, it is not uncommon when they are home for a visit for them to come squeeze in between Juliette and me when we are reading or watching a show in bed to have a quick talk or just to connect before saying goodnight. I think the birth of my children has similarly freed me to be more demonstrative with my mother than I ever had been.

I firmly believe that my mother's life would have been very different had she not gone to live with Aunt Elizabeth as a child and attended the schools in the city. As a matter of fact, it is very possible she might not have gone to college where she met my father. Had she not, I might not have been born. For as much as I idolize Mama Ceal and for as much as I consider her "my person," I also know that there are aspects of my personality that were very much shaped by Aunt Elizabeth (Momo) and the fact that I too lived in her house as a small child. I would not have spent the first few years of my life taking in the peculiar ways of Momo's fastidiousness and personal discipline and love of being very well dressed whenever I left the house. I might not have developed the traits that have influenced my work ethic, the way I carry myself in professional settings, the way I have constructed my person. The list of "might nots" and "would nots" is almost endless but the point is clear: decisions made long before I was born or thought of have reverberated for generations to influence who, what, and where I am today.

I love the concept of "standing on the shoulders" of those who came before us as it acknowledges that but for the efforts of our forebearers, we would be in a very different and less advantageous posture. What is not readily apparent when we invoke that image is that what we are actually doing is, in addition to standing on the foundations of our ancestors' achievements, we are also standing on the platforms of their suffering, suffering that is just as critical as the achievements. In addition to the overwhelming gratitude I feel for the sacrifices, it is difficult not to also feel some measure of guilt and to question whether I deserve it.

It seems odd though that life demanded as sacrifice the strain that existed between Mama Ceal and my mother, and the awkwardness that affected my mother's ability to show more affection to my sister and me in order for us to be in the place we are now. It is also uncomfortable to acknowledge — and makes me wonder if I'm being selfish — that although I wish I could have spared my grandmother and mother the pain that resulted from the choices they made, I wouldn't change any of it if it meant my now wouldn't be what it is. Maybe the inheritance of my deep abiding love for Mama Ceal and the heirloom quilts and the ritual of chocolate coconut balls at Christmas could only exist if accompanied by the inheritance of that pain and estrangement and awkwardness that we all felt to some degree. There is a poignancy in that realization, but in my grandmother's words: this leaves me okay.

TWENTY

More than once, Lucille had to remind herself to focus on the clothes she was folding as she kept getting lost in her thoughts. As the radio played in the background, she continued to turn over in her head that in a few months, LaRuth was graduating from high school. She almost voiced out loud: "Lord, how could that be?" While there were periods over the years when she was apart from LaRuth that time seemed to drag on, it still felt like this moment had come upon her suddenly and in a way that made her feel not fully prepared. Had they really reached the year 1959 and LaRuth's impending graduation?

Just the year before, Lucille had heard about and quietly celebrated the graduation of Ernest Green as the first of the nine Negro students who integrated Little Rock Central High School. She had seen the reports on the Hortons' TV and the news had been filled with stories about the "crisis" as they had called it. Those were uncomfortable moments when she happened to be watching with the Hortons during those news reports because she wasn't sure how the Hortons felt about the whole thing. Other than hearing Mr. Lee express one evening: "what a mess," the Hortons had not said whether they thought what was happening was a good thing or a bad thing. Was his disgust with integration or the people protesting it or with the poor way it was being handled? She couldn't imagine Mr. Lee or Mrs. Della being part of the crowd demonstrating and yelling to keep those students out of that school but she also didn't know how they might feel if it was the local White school that was being integrated. How would they have felt if LaRuth was the one integrating?

As far as she was concerned, Lucille hadn't trusted Arkansas' governor, Orval Faubus. While he said repeatedly that he was trying to protect everyone, the way he talked made it clear to her that he didn't really want integration. Plus, from what she had seen, it didn't seem like the "everyone" he was trying to protect included those Black students. She had prayed that God kept those brave children safe and she prayed for their parents who had to be going through so much fear and worry over their babies. She knew she would be. Fortunately, none of them had been harmed — at least not physically.

As she took another towel from the clothes basket, she couldn't help but gasp when hearing the latest news break coming over the radio. The radio announcer was saying that 21 boys between the ages of 13 and 17 at the Negro Boys Industrial School had burned to death. "Lord, have mercy" is all that Lucille could repeat to herself as she listened to the report. Located in Wrightsville, just south of Little Rock, the "reform school" was set up to house orphaned and homeless Negro boys as well as those who had been deemed delinquent because of a variety of crimes, some of which were as minor as riding a White boy's bike or engaging in a Halloween prank.

In reality, the institution operated more as a junior prison/industrial work farm that in no way resembled the state's White reform schools. The latter instead focused on educational objectives and treated its residents like students who were taught vocational skills such as carpentry, metal work, bricklaying, tailoring, shoe mending, plastering and the like. In the segregated Negro reform school, the boys performed farm work in the surrounding fields and were subject to cruel conditions, including being whipped with a leather strap for infractions, going without sufficient clothes, socks and underwear, and not even having safe drinking water. Apparently, the boys had been locked in their dormitories as was the nightly practice to ensure no one escaped, although the White schools did not lock dormitory doors at night and ensured house parents were on duty. When a fire started in the building, 48 boys managed to escape, but the remaining 21 could not.

Lucille said a prayer for those boys and their families and willed herself to think about other things, like her gratitude that LaRuth did not have to be in either a reform school or, for that matter, the little country school she was supposed to attend had she not gone to live with Elizabeth. "Thank you, Jesus," she whispered. They all were fortunate that they had been spared such tragedy and heartache.

If the years to LaRuth's senior year in high school passed quickly, the few months leading up to graduation flew by even more rapidly. Lucille found herself in the midst of a whirlwind of commencement activities associated with LaRuth's completion of her high school education.

The first part of her dream that had been conceived more than a decade before was coming to fruition. There were several programs leading up to the graduation ceremony itself. Come hell or high water, Lucille was determined to be at every one. She had notified the Hortons well in advance that she was planning to take time to attend LaRuth's graduation activities, one of the few times she was confident in making a declaration rather than a request. Fortunately, there were other families in Newcastle who had students graduating so she was able to get a ride into town for each event. She was also grateful when Mr. Lee told her he would take her or have someone take her into Forrest City if she couldn't otherwise find a way.

The commencement activities started with a baccalaureate service in the school gymnasium. The program was held Sunday afternoon to allow folks to attend their regular worship services that morning. The school choir had rehearsed for over a month to meet the director's aim that the singers be perfect in their renditions of their selections which included the "Star Spangled Banner" and a special arrangement of a familiar hymn. Perhaps she was already emotional with the start of the week's activities but the lyrics of the Negro National Anthem — "Lift Every Voice and Sing" — felt particularly meaningful to her that day.

Sing a song full of the faith that the dark past has taught us. Sing a song full of the hope the present has brought us . . . Have not our weary feet come to the place for which our fathers sighed? . . . Out from the gloomy past, till now we stand at last where the white gleam of our bright star is cast.

She focused on every part of the program as she had waited a long time for this moment. She guessed that the local minister who delivered the homily complied with the instructions to keep his message dignified and appropriate for the occasion without any hooping or too much "spirit." Overall, it was a brief but touching service and a good way to begin the celebrations.

The Monday night program was slightly less formal although the students had been admonished by the teachers and administrators that they would brook no foolishness or shenanigans. The threat of a withheld diploma was more than effective at discouraging mischief as none of the graduates risked facing the repercussions such embarrassment could bring to their families. The program included remarks from administrators and teachers and featured members of the senior class presenting songs, readings, skits, and acknowledgements.

On Wednesday evening, the school held a social with dancing and refreshments. Lucille thought all of the boys and girls looked so nice in their suits and dresses. And she was happy to get a chance to meet some of LaRuth's teachers whom she had not met. She was proud that she could contribute some of her pecan sandies for the reception and, from the looks of things, people must have really enjoyed them because they were one of the items that was all gone before the conclusion of the night. Lucille could tell that Elizabeth wasn't a huge fan of the dance but she was able to hide her disdain from everyone else. For the students, the music and dancing were bland compared to the James Brown, Sam Cooke, LaVern Baker, and Jackie Wilson numbers they preferred, but it was all part of the choreography to get their ultimate goal: official liberation from high school and its many restrictions and limitations.

On Thursday night, the graduates were saluted by a keynote speaker and received their diplomas and awards. While LaRuth seemed happy though underwhelmed by it all, the whole week had been special for Lucille. However, Thursday night when diplomas were given was an especially proud moment for her. She could not stop smiling even as she occasionally dabbed her eyes with the neatly pressed handkerchief in her pocketbook. She thought of the fact that she only completed the eighth grade. Of course, she thought of Walter and of their agonizing decision to send LaRuth to live with Elizabeth. She thought about the night Walter drowned and how tempted she was to bring LaRuth home. She thought about the nights she had cried herself to sleep wishing that her only child was there with her. She thought about how conflicted she was in both appreciating Elizabeth for letting LaRuth come live with her and resenting Elizabeth for the time and moments with LaRuth that Lucille would never have. A flood of memories had overtaken her as she also recognized that the realization of her dream for her daughter had come at a significant cost. Nothing could erase the longing for more time with LaRuth growing up that she continued to hold deep inside. Still, Lucille was certain that it had been a good decision and she knew to hold on tight to that feeling to help ameliorate the loss and deprivation she had experienced.

"I know you is happy glad right now," Dessie Mae whispered to Lucille as she grasped her sister's hand and scooted a little closer as LaRuth descended the steps of the stage.

"You know I am," Lucille replied this time, not bothering to capture the lone tear that had escaped her vigilance.

"I know how hard it was for you to let her be with Elizabeth," Dessie added, giving Lucille's hand an extra squeeze.

All Lucille could do was press her lips together and squeeze her sister's hand in return since to say or do anything more threatened to unleashed more emotion and tears than she could manage.

She wondered whether LaRuth would notice that she had made herself a new outfit for the occasion. She felt proud of the blue crepe dress that the Butterick pattern had described as "elegant and tasteful in its simplicity." Lucille didn't like a lot of embellishments anyway, but she also didn't want to take away the focus from LaRuth. After all, it was her day. She assumed Elizabeth's suit was new too; it was indeed very smart and matched her coordinating hat, purse and gloves. Lucille pulled her pocketbook a little closer to her and resolved that she would try to get herself a new one once LaRuth was settled in college. She also noted that Elizabeth looked especially proud, like many of the other mothers of graduates looked. Lucille hoped that her older accessories didn't embarrass LaRuth. Just as quickly as the thought entered her head, she chided herself for letting these petty ideas try to detract from the joy of the day and her own sense of accomplishment. "Fix my mind, Jesus," she thought to herself and smiled even wider as she focused on the closing benediction.

In that moment, Lucille knew that everything was about to change even more than she had anticipated. She had not expected LaRuth to "come home" to her in Newcastle, but it was clear now that any chance of that happening was gone. Her baby was about to step into adulthood. She was happy for the achievement but couldn't suppress the pang of sadness that it represented as well.

There were plenty of folks there to greet both LaRuth and her cousin Dene as they made their way from the front of the gym after the ceremony. Lucille had contented herself to see LaRuth once she got through the throng of family and friends. But she could not hold her tears when LaRuth made a beeline directly to her, past the other family members and friends to bestow her first hug as a high school graduate, and to whisper in her ear, "I like your new dress. It's pretty."

TWENTY-ONE

"What a beautiful day," Lucille thought to herself as she walked the hundred odd feet from Lee and Della Horton's home to that of their son Eugene, his wife Marian, and their sons John and Carl. The air had turned crisp. Although there had been several cool days lately, this day felt mild. The leaves were falling in a steady, albeit random, way and almost covered the ground completely. A breeze caused the swings near the house to rock slightly and their chains to squeak just enough to add some texture to an otherwise quiet, serene lunch hour.

She could find something to love about almost every time of year. She wasn't a huge fan of winter's cold, but Christmas was her favorite holiday with all the gift-giving, baking, and general goodwill. It was uplifting to see her flowers and plantings beginning to sprout in the spring. People's moods seemed much lighter and easier in the summer. But the fall of 1959 — during the period just after the heat had died down and before there was a big drop in temperature that necessitated more than a light jacket — felt like the return of an old friend. With school a few months in session and routines set, there was time to take stock and contemplate matters both reassuring and comforting as well as poignant and unsettling, thoughts that might often get crowded out due to the press of life at other times of the year.

Lucille helped Mr. Gene and Ms. Marian one or two days a week, depending on their needs and what she had to do for Mr. Lee and Ms. Della. On this particular day, Lee Horton had gone to town on some errand and Della was in the middle of reading her lesson in preparation for the next night's Bible study. Eugene Horton was at his job with the state highway commission. Marian was off shopping with a lady from her church and John and Carl were at school but returning home in a few hours. The house was quiet and Lucille could get through the light housekeeping of straightening up the main living area and kitchen easily enough. She had agreed to watch the boys later when Gene and Marian had to go out so she was happy that this was not the week she was expected to do additional tasks like cleaning the bathroom or changing the linen. Today, she could focus on the ironing, the most time-consuming of tasks she did for Ms. Marian.

"Now, Lucille, you really shouldn't sit while you are ironing, understand?" Marian had directed one day. "You have to stand up to iron properly."

"Yes, ma'am," Lucille replied calmly, belying her true thoughts or intentions regarding the instruction. Not that she was lazy or preferred to sit while ironing. But she knew that if she was tired and needed to sit to finish her work out of Marian Horton's presence, she would do so. Plus, she figured she could count on one hand the number of things that Ms. Marian had ironed. Lucille imagined Marian had probably heard her mother or grandmother say that to some other Negro maid and adopted the position as gospel regarding running an appropriate Southern home. It seemed, Ms. Marian rarely missed an opportunity to remind Lucille who was in charge.

Nevertheless, she refused to give the remembrance of that exchange the luxury of much thought or even slight annoyance. Today, Lucille was determined to maintain her equanimity. Although she was already missing LaRuth, she held tight to the idea that her daughter was away *in college.*

The summer weeks after LaRuth's graduation had rushed by in a haze. LaRuth had spent the time babysitting and cleaning house for a white family in Forrest City to save money for school so she didn't get out to Newcastle as often as either of them wanted before it was time for her to leave. Lucille wasn't thrilled about LaRuth working as a maid, but she knew it was only temporary — she could stand for her to do it now so that she didn't have to do it later — and the money was definitely needed to help LaRuth get ready for college and cover her upcoming expenses.

Arkansas Agricultural, Mechanical & Normal College in Pine Bluff, AM&N as it was more popularly known, was where LaRuth would matriculate. It wasn't her first choice as she had also been accepted to Tougaloo College in Jackson, Mississippi. However, her mother, Aunt Elizabeth and she, though reluctantly, all agreed that the family could not afford for her to attend school there. It was already going to be an effort to get everything together for her to attend any school, but they were determined that she was going to college and the historically Black college two hours from Forrest City had a solid reputation. Although she hated to disappoint LaRuth, Lucille was not at all upset that Pine

Bluff was closer than Jackson.

The trip to take LaRuth to school was sad and exciting: sad because it was going to be hard to say goodbye but also exciting since Lucille had never been to a college campus before. Other than Elizabeth's occasional comment about other drivers, no one talked much in the car. Lucille felt that LaRuth must have been a little disappointed that Owen had not joined them on the trip. Instead, LaRuth's Uncle "Po'ter," Elizabeth's half-brother Elporter Gamble, had driven them since Owen did not want to miss work.

As the highway narrowed and turned into more of a street, it was clear they were coming into town. Because they were traveling south to Pine Bluff, they had entered the city on its north side, where the college was the first real landmark to command your attention. When LaRuth pointed out the AM&N sign at the beginning of the campus, Lucille paid special attention to take in as much as she could about this place that her daughter would be calling home for the next several years.

There was a football stadium on one side of the street that looked like some of the ones she had seen on TV with the Hortons. To think this one was for Negro students! On the other side of the street were a ton of buildings, more than she could count as they passed. She could see open spaces and sidewalks among the trees and buildings. How long would it take LaRuth to learn her way around?

Elporter followed the signs directing new students to their dormitories and registration stations. As she was able to take in more of it, Lucille thought the campus looked beautiful. There were flowers planted at various places and the lawn appeared as if it had just been cut. Although it startled her the first time it rang, she enjoyed the sound of the bell that marked each quarter hour. She had seen the bell tower from the car but didn't know what it was until someone explained it later. Lucille wasn't sure how many blocks they had gone before turning onto a street that took them into the campus and then onto another one that led to the dormitories. This place looked like a small town by itself. It was certainly bigger than Newcastle. A man directing traffic guided them to the buildings that were the girls' dormitories which were across the street from the boys' dormitories.

"Well that's good that they have the boys separate from the girls," Elizabeth commented to no one in particular.

As they parked, Lucille's eyes widened at the number of students, all of them dressed very nicely, perhaps not as nice as church but still respectable. Like her, Elizabeth and Elporter, there were lots of families trying to help get their students moved in. Some of the families were nice and shared the little bits of information they had gathered — like where to go first; who to ask for help; how to find the restrooms — with those who looked lost or overwhelmed by it all. Lucille learned that many of them had come from small communities like she had. A few other families were a lot less friendly — and a lot more sedity. Lucille assumed that this was not their first time being at a college. She saw how they looked down their noses at other folks and seemed annoyed when asked for help. Lucille shook her head. If she had managed not to let Elizabeth's ticky ways get under her skin, she certainly was not about to let these snooty people she didn't even know do so.

While Lucille could feel her anxiousness rising, LaRuth seemed calm and more self-assured than Lucille had ever seen her. Her daughter who apparently had become a young lady focused on the directions for what she needed to do and where she needed to go while also reassuring her family that she could handle things.

The three of them waited at the car while LaRuth was directed to a line for a registration table to confirm everything was in order. Lucille got a bit nervous as the time ticked by; she had seen some girls come back to their families distressed that some form or payment was missing. She breathed a sigh of relief when LaRuth came back and reported that she had delivered the folded envelope with the check to pay her family's contribution and received the receipt along with her room assignment and class schedule.

As they moved LaRuth into her dormitory room, Lucille was content to let Elizabeth fuss with getting the bed made while she and LaRuth put away the clothes that they could fit in her chest of drawers and then put the rest in her footlocker that sat at the end of her bed. She smiled to herself as Elizabeth folded and smoothed the fan quilt she had labored over a few years earlier on top of the bedspread.

With her fees paid, her room organized, and an assembly for new students she was to attend shortly, along with a desire on her family's part to get home before dark, it was time for LaRuth's contingency to prepare to return to Forrest City.

"Thank you for helping me get settled in," LaRuth said to her family as she started to bid them farewell. "Thank you for driving us, Uncle Po'ter."

He nodded, gave her a side embrace, and turned to the car without a word.

"Now remember your home training," admonished Elizabeth as she gave LaRuth a quick, polite hug. "Don't let your name beat you back home."

"Yes, ma'am," LaRuth replied.

"I love you," Lucille whispered to her daughter. "I wish it was more," she continued as she pushed a few folded dollars into LaRuth's hand.

"Thank you, mama. I love you, too," LaRuth smiled back, a little thrown off trying to remember the last time her mother had said that.

"We better get going," Elizabeth called back as she opened the car door.

Lucille had expected to feel more upset as she said goodbye but she kept her resolve to tamp down any rising emotions, which she could indulge back in Newcastle. She was glad that LaRuth didn't appear nervous. Did their hug seem a little harder and longer than usual? Lucille wasn't sure but she liked the idea that it might have been, which made the ride home a lot easier.

Recalling it now, Lucille felt proud of how well she handled herself.

"I guess I was a big girl after all," she sighed.

Noticing the time, she remembered that she still needed to finish dinner for Mr. Lee and Ms. Della, and had also agreed to watch the boys when Mr. Gene and Ms. Marian went out to their friends' home. Adjusting the height of the ironing board, she sat down to iron the three remaining shirts.

TWENTY-TWO

Route 1 Bx 315
Forrest City Ark

Dear Walter
 Well this is to let you here from me this leve me all hope you and Juliette is ok, give my Love to here fore me oh Bam Bam Day He also Selmer and tove you to be a good boy oh Neu Casel is billen up The man That Werk fore John have moved a tralor up on the hill Just across from the white house before you come down the Hill to the gin. Well Mrs Hella is not eny Better so its the Lady that Stay at night she is real nice
Love moma e.

> *Route 1 Box 315*
> *Forrest City, Ark*
> > *Dear Walter*
> > *Well this is to let you here from me. This leve me ok. Hope you and Juliette is ok. Give my love to here fore me. Oh Bam Bam say hi also Selma and fore you to be a good boy. Oh New Casel is billen up. The man that work fore John have moved a tralur up on the hill just across from the white house before you come down the hill to the gin. Well Mrs. Della is not any better so it's the lady that stay at night. She is real nice*
> > *love Moma C.*

The other day, my daughter shared in our family group chat a screenshot of a Twitter post she had recently come across. The tweet was a quote by Toni Morrison on love and generations:

> *Each generation has a kind of love. Some of it's really tough. What my grandmother thought was love of her children was really staying alive for them. What my mother thought was love of her children was to get a better place, maybe get enough money to send you to college if you wanted to. What I thought was love of my children was giving them the maximum amount of freedom, setting an example of how you could make choices in your life.*

As I think about the quote, I can't help but get both sad and angry at the idea that the life of Morrison's grandmother, like so many Black ancestors — like my ancestors — was so grueling, so demoralizing, so soul-crushing that the most she could do to express her love for her children was to stay alive. I imagine the deprivation that both mother and children experienced at not holding or being held and comforted, perhaps not saying or hearing expressions of loving words, not having the security or reassurance of being affirmed as deserving love. Is there a point at which a child realizes that the touch, the nurturing, the sense of being wanted that she yearns for will not be felt? Or does that unmet desire morph into something else, be it positive or negative, motivating or self-destructive? And what about the child who doesn't know to see his mother's effort to stay alive as the only expression of love she is capable of extending?

For my grandmother, sending her daughter to live with her bossy sister-cousin was an expression of love. I doubt my grandmother gave a lot of thought to whether her daughter was old enough to understand that her mother's sacrifice was one of the highest expressions of love that she could offer. She believed that the ability for her daughter to have a better life was dependent upon getting a better education than she could get at the rural school she would have attended. But what my grandmother hadn't realized is that she could have made this situation easier for her daughter — and maybe herself — if she had just explained to my mother how much she loved her and how hard it was to send her to live with someone else. It's also possible that the pain my grandmother felt at sending her daughter away was too great for her to acknowledge. Perhaps instead, she swallowed her hurt and longing and — unfortunately and unknowingly — communicated to her daughter that there wasn't any. Even as I can understand if that were the case, the question remains whether that's a good enough reason.

It is easy for me to look back now and question why Mama Ceal didn't explain everything to my mother. The temptation to judge through my lens how easy and simple it all could have been, however, fails to take into account the times and social mores that shaped my grandmother. As a child and an adult, Lucille was acculturated to believe that children were to be seen and not heard. The idea of explaining things to children or even considering their opinions was not a widely held concept. In most instances, adults didn't feel the need to explain situations to children or ask them what they thought. Children were to speak when spoken to but otherwise remain quiet and compliant. The same was true for me as a child although those ideas had started to give way to new thoughts in some circles, partly due to changing ideas projected on television and partly due to the growing focus on "parenting" literature and the popularity of childcare experts like Benjamin Spock. (To be clear, my family was not among those in such circles when I was growing up.)

Understandably, Aunt Elizabeth/Momo, too, shared a similar outlook that it wasn't necessary to explain the why of anything to children as much as it was to mold them to be the adults one expected them to become. Her wholehearted adoption of the concept of not spoiling a child caused her to miss the opportunity to create more of a maternal bond with my mother as she dutifully raised her. She all but hid the love she held for my mother.

That my mother experienced a certain alienation from the two central maternal figures in her life makes me sad. For as much as I absolutely adored Mama Ceal and loved Momo, and in spite of my knaowledge that they both did the best they could with the skills and understanding that they had at the time, I can't help but also be disappointed that neither of them had the presence of mind to love my mother in the way that she really needed.

As a result, my mother became skilled at swallowing her hurt and feelings. She never expressed to her mother how much she'd rather be with her than to live with her Aunt Elizabeth. Perhaps she assumed there was no point in telling her mother how much she missed her. The few times she had asked to stay with her mother, she was met with the same response: she was better off at the better school. I believe the first time that my mother ever said out loud that she didn't feel better off was when I was an adult asking her about what it was like to have to live away from her mother. It was then that she shared with me that she just felt like her mother had sent her away and never seemed to be too bothered by it. Similarly, my mother hardly ever spoke up to Aunt Elizabeth to defend herself or question her treatment or the decisions that seemed harsh or unfair. Besides the fact that she was the child, my mother wasn't equipped nor did circumstances or culture allow her to be more of an advocate for herself. And it seems unreasonable to expect her to make up for the lapses of adults.

As a kid, I shared my mother's tendency to defer to the authority of the adults in my life, specifically my parents and family elders. The idea of contradicting an adult was practically unheard of as a small child. I was a teenager before I reached a point at which I was brave enough to openly "disagree" with my father. That disagreement amounted to basically one "argument" that revolved around the real-world impact of daylight savings time. It happened only because I was convinced that on that topic, I was one hundred percent right and somehow felt empowered to express my differing view. (Suffice it to say my position rested on the practical aspect of what happens when you move a clock forward or backward an hour while my dad's argument was based on whether you technically "gain" or "lose" an hour on the clock.)

To be fair, in looking back, my mother has shared with me that Mama Ceal did try to show affection to her in a number of other ways. Mama Ceal called occasionally and took advantage of Mrs. Della's trips to town to visit when she could. She made special treats for my mother when she came to visit. Still, they both carried a lot of emotional wounds. For my grandmother, I believe some of the wounds from which she operated were partly due to my grandfather's death. For my mother, Mama Ceal and Momo, I suspect the wounds that shaped their relationships were partly due to their failure to communicate and partly due to the constraint of cultural norms and customs, the disadvantages of which had grown to outweigh their benefits.

In spite of the hardships and emotional scars they carried, the truth is the decision to have my mother attend school in Forrest City was probably the best. The likelihood of my mother going to college without question would not have been as great had she stayed in the rural school. Attending Arkansas AM & N College was indeed life-changing for my mother, as college experiences usually are for all students. It was while she was in college that she met lifelong friends, and discovered her interest in teaching, and met my father. As the objective was to provide more opportunities and possibilities for my mother, the experiment was a success. My grandmother's goal was realized.

The unfortunate part is that it came at a high emotional price — "those things we lost in the fire."

But to stop there reduces the analysis to a false dichotomy. The emotional price did not necessarily have to be so high: the choice did not have to be better education and trauma or subpar education and emotional security. The benefits of getting a better education that prepared her for and motivated her to attend college did not necessarily have to come at the expense of my mother's emotional wellbeing. She could very well have gone to live in Forrest City to attend school and still had Mama Ceal and Momo extend themselves more to make sure she was okay. They could have considered how she may have felt and how they could have been more supportive.

I recognize that it's due to the price they paid that I am where and who I am today. Their sacrifices, their hurts, their pains and disappointments all shaped them and, in turn, influenced the parents and grandparents they were to me. Their experiences shaped me as well. There are times that I feel guilty about what they had to go through in order for me to be who I am. I suppose this is much the same way I feel bad about the emotional injuries from which I wish I could save my children. But the fact of the matter is, I have no responsibility for what my parents and grandparents endured. Similarly, I shouldn't be able to shield my children from disappointment — including the ones I cause them — since to do so I believe could cripple them in their ability to succeed as adults. Though difficult, I have come to accept that dynamic and come to some degree of peace with it.

Fortunately, there are many more instances in which I am grateful than I am regretful for the influences of my family's experiences. Mama Ceal's gregariousness and ability to make people comfortable in her presence has to be in my genes even if it may have been a recessive trait in my mother. Despite Mama

Ceal's seeming subservience, she possessed a certain confidence and self-assuredness that I suspect was foreign to many Black people of the time. While she was the Hortons' maid, she believed herself to be part of their family. I believed her to be, too. As a result, I didn't experience the discomfort or uneasiness some of my childhood friends felt in the presence of White people. Life later taught me other reasons I might have to be careful in "mixed" company, but I started with the idea that I was as important as any White person, not because my parents or family told me so but because it was what I believed I saw. And I was — at least initially — oblivious to the class difference between White employer and Black help. That exposure and early mindset played a role in how I saw myself then and how I show up in the spaces I inhabit now.

Momo's fastidiousness and well-mannered affect also found their way into my psyche. A neighbor who lived down the street from her said: "Miss Whitley would always make sure you kids were as clean as the board of health whenever you left that house. I had never seen such clean, well-behaved and well-dressed children before." I'm sure, to this day, that has something to do with the fact that my "casual" is rarely as casual as my friends even when we may be doing nothing but hanging around the house. Momo's straitlaced primness impacts how I carry myself in professional settings and likely has benefited me in ways I have taken for granted even as I found them overbearing and tiresome when I was younger.

Mama Ceal showed love by recognizing that she could give her daughter an advantage in life by sending her to a better school and planting the idea of going to college. Whether she was trying to simply hold it together to survive the pain of allowing another woman to raise her child or instead was putting on a brave face and not sharing how that decision impacted her so as not to upset her daughter, she undercut her message of love for my mother.

Momo showed love by steadfastly focusing on the mechanics of raising a respectable young Negro woman to ensure that her life could be better than those whom Momo considered common and who didn't appreciate the importance of appearance and impression. If my mother was clean and articulate enough, White people would be compelled to treat her better. Momo didn't appreciate that trying to distance my mother from the stereotypical and disrespected aspects of her community could not shield her from the insidiousness of systemic racism that she still faced.

My mother showed love to my sister and me by trying to give us moments in our childhood of which she often felt deprived. She made sure to take us to the carnival, to make special meals for our birthdays; and to allow us to order drinks when we grabbed fast food without my father (as he felt it was a waste of money to buy the over-priced pop or milkshakes). She even made efforts to overcome her discomfort with showing emotion and affection by occasionally giving us back rubs on nights when we couldn't fall asleep.

Understandably, digging through family history and dynamics and exploring old wounds can be unsettling, jarring, upsetting. I have found it at times both poignant and disappointing when I have had to come face to face with the humanness and fallibility of revered loved ones, especially Mama Ceal. The undertaking though has given me an opportunity to explore my own failings and shortcomings, as a son, husband, parent, family member. If nothing else, I am learning to apply more broadly to others the grace and understanding that I am often quick to extend myself. I am learning to value the bumps and bruises, the failures and slights, and the disappointments and low points almost as much as I celebrate the accomplishments, successes, and triumphs that are mine and my family's.

As I think about this idea of how families show love across generations and the impact of those shortcomings, I can't help but consider how those dynamics have played out with my children. I contrast my unquestioned deference to adults with my children who seemed to come out of the womb challenging conventions and idioms that I had taken as given but for which they required full explanation and support. For sure, what we thought was love was to talk to our children as adults almost from birth. Where my grandmother explained nothing, we explained practically everything. We solicited their feelings and input, not to necessarily dictate our decisions but to help them understand why we did what we did so that they felt they had the right to be seen and heard.

Our shorthand for our daughter Adjua's outlook is that she is the savior of and advocate for every marginalized person and "broken-winged bird" she comes across. That finds expression, by way of example, in her staunch defense of restaurant workers who may offer less than exemplary service as she reminds us of how grueling and unappreciated their work is and how unaware we are of what might be impacting them at a particular moment as they struggle to do their jobs. We joke that if a server poured a pitcher of water over her head, her first response would most likely be: "But what do you think he must be experiencing right now to make him do that?" She is relentless in pressing us to put ourselves in the place of others whom we are tempted to critique or judge and who don't share the privilege we enjoy as a practical way to live out our early lessons of the importance of kindness.

"Okay you two — what's the status of finding therapists?" read a text on my phone not too long ago. Our son Wade Osei was dogged in cajoling, nagging, nudging, reminding and doing whatever he could to make us keep the promise we made. One of our many "life in the time of Covid" family discussions centered on the importance of mental health and emotional care. Both children made impassioned pleas for us to treat our emotional health with the same seriousness that we treated our physical health, stressing the importance of regular maintenance and the value of exploring unacknowledged (and undiagnosed) conditions. The result of that discussion was a commitment on the part of Juliette and myself to find and see therapists. Both kids had begun seeing therapists years ago, but outside of pre-marital counseling and a marriage "checkup," we had not. Of course, they were right: we have found therapy to be really wonderful at helping us carve out time to center ourselves, focus on self-awareness goals, and explore patterns we hadn't realized we were repeating.

If nothing else, I feel we achieved our goal of impressing upon our children their ability to develop their own sense of self and their right to be seen and heard. They certainly are not hesitant to make their opinions and positions known. However, the clearest and most gratifying expression of them exercising such agency is in how they demonstrate love. They have such an absolute confidence in love that it makes them fearless in addressing issues and family dynamics that prior generations avoided out of politeness, a sense of decorum, or a sense of protecting others' feelings. Theirs is a world that trusts love can conquer any hurt or discomfort. Thus, there are no taboo topics; there are no swallowed hurts; there are no unacknowledged slights. They believe in openness and transparency (perhaps sharing more than I care to know sometimes). They believe in telling you when you have hurt them, not to indict or chastise, but to create pathways for healing. They ask awkward questions and raise sensitive issues. And even when there are tears, bruised feelings, and heated exchanges as a result of these courageous conversations, we almost always look back and feel that we are the better for having had the experience and appreciate the sense of having a weight lifted because we have finally addressed a concern that was being ignored or avoided.

I once went to hear Angela Davis speak and recall her saying that failing to teach children about racism is like sending them outside in a rainstorm without an umbrella. In the same way that we struggled to figure out how to address issues like racism, I think of the many other difficult lessons and aspects of life that we have had to share with our children and wonder how those instances speak to the ways we showed love. Did the way that we showed love mean that we had some conversations too early, making them wonder about their right to take up space or doubt the validity of their dreams. Did we wait too late to teach other lessons, making them question the self-esteem we had tried to instill in them or less confident in what they thought they believed?

As I imagine Mama Ceal and Momo may have also felt, we try to take some comfort in believing we did the best that we could. But the questions always linger: Was it enough? Was it too much? What have been the unintended consequences of our well-intentioned actions?

I do know deep in my heart that the kind of love that my children will show toward their children will be one that is patient, grounding, forgiving, honest, and courageous. I am confident of this because that is the kind of adults I am proud to see them becoming. Their ways of expressing love build upon what has come from the generations before them. And, like those ancestors, they will show love in the best ways that they know how.

TWENTY-THREE

There was something about the smell of baking at Christmas that was more special, more magical for Lucille than at any other time of the year. Even items she might make throughout the year took on an added charm when done at Christmas. She was especially pleased with the batch of oatmeal raisin cookies she had just taken out of the oven. Both John and Carl had asked her to make something that they could take to school for their class Christmas parties. Carl wanted peppermint fudge — which Lucille suspected was to impress one of the little girls in his fourth-grade class that he had a crush on. It was already in the refrigerator cooling with crushed peppermint sitting prominently atop the rich chocolate confection. John had chosen oatmeal cookies for the seventh-grade celebration and these smelled wonderful. The cinnamon was always the first scent she could detect but then the smell of vanilla and cloves, followed by butter and brown sugar had filled the kitchen, bringing a smile to her face in the process. Once they cooled, Lucille would pack them in wax paper in one of the holiday tins from last year.

The holidays also meant that LaRuth came home. It was hard to believe that this was now her third Christmas break in college. "Coming home" meant that she went to Elizabeth's from Pine Bluff — this year getting a ride home with a schoolmate from Forrest City — and then she would see Lucille after spending a couple of days with Elizabeth and depending on who was available to bring her to Newcastle.

The three years that LaRuth spent in college hadn't necessarily rushed by, but Lucille knew that the time could have felt like a real ordeal had she not had the Horton boys to help look after. Oh, how she loved those boys. They seemed to adore her as well. She laughed remembering their antics over the years as she transferred the cookies to the cooling rack.

There was the bath time Carl offered to marry her so that she wouldn't be lonely. With Mr. Gene and Ms. Marian enjoying an evening out during the week, Lucille was getting the boys ready for bed in anticipation of their parents' return. Water seemed to be everywhere except the bathtub as the boys had splashed themselves silly. How Lucille had managed to stay mostly dry was a miracle. The mountain of bubbles they created after adding more bubble bath to the running water when Lucille turned her back was long gone and half the toys scattered on the floor.

"Bobo?" questioned Carl as he played with the remaining suds in the tub, delaying his exit. "Why did your husband die?"

"I don't know," Lucille answered. "I guess the good Lord decided it was time for him to come home."

Lucille could tell that the wheels were still turning inside his head and that more questions were likely.

"You finish up rinsing off the rest of those soap suds so you can get out of the tub," she coaxed. "John is almost dry already."

As the older sibling by three years, eight-year-old John had just asked Lucille why he had to take his bath with his younger brother — and with her supervision. Her quick response that maybe he was ready to have his own bath time was met with a pleased smile.

"Bobo, ain't you lonely without a husband?" Carl continued. "You ever gonna get another one?"

"No, sirree," Lucille chuckled, responding to the last question. "I don't plan on having no more husbands. And I don't have time to be lonely. I got LaRuth —"

"But she's all the way in Pine Bluff in college!" he interrupted.

"And I got you and John, and your mama and daddy, and your Pawpaw Lee and Mawmaw Della to look after."

"Well, I'll marry you when I get bigger so you can have a husband," Carl declared.

"You can't marry Bobo, silly," John chided his brother. "She's —"

Both Carl and Lucille immediately looked up at John, each anxious to hear what he was going to say, Carl chafing at his older sibling's reprimand, and Lucille unsure whether John's kind nature had been tainted by some of the other boys at school.

"—too old," John finished.

"And you are right about it," Lucille responded before Carl could retort. "Hang up your towel and get your teeth brushed. Carl, let's get you dry and in your pajamas so you can get yours brushed, too."

She thought of the four-leaf clovers that John had collected for her over the years that she kept pressed in her Bible. She smiled remembering how tickled they got when they could sneak up behind her and untie her apron strings before she realized they were there. Her bluffs to chase them up a tree or skin them alive were met with squeals of delight.

There was the day that she crushed both boys' excitement as she hung out the laundry on the clothesline while the boys played nearby. John and Carl had not realized that their inability to whisper, coupled with Lucille's many years of gardening, made their plan to scare her with the squirmy garden snake they found likely unsuccessful. Her offer to cook it for them for dinner was met with a pair of disappointed harrumphs followed by bellyaching laughter from all three of them.

The times that she was asked to watch John and Carl might have otherwise felt like an added burden, but Lucille's love for them made her childcare duties the easiest of her list of chores. Sure, the boys could be a handful, but they energized her as much as they drained her. Moreover, almost every bath time, joint cookie-baking, and scraped-knee tending gave her time to be the mother she otherwise had been able to be only in discrete pockets with LaRuth. Even as she took joy in those moments, they also served as painful reminders that she didn't have nearly as many of them with her own child. The bulk of LaRuth's childhood had been spent in someone else's care. In Elizabeth's care. While she was eager for the opportunities to mind Carl and John, those opportunities also made her vulnerable to the poignant reminders that she missed so many similar moments with LaRuth.

Fortunately, the holidays offered periods where Lucille could spend more time with LaRuth, the main reason that made Christmas special. For years they had maintained a holiday tradition that gave them more uninterrupted time together, time that they both enjoyed and looked forward to. On the day after Christmas, mother and daughter either took the bus or sometimes Lucille paid someone to drive them to her father Tommy's house in Casscoe. They would then spend the week between Christmas and New Year's Day with him. The visits always began with Lucille buying groceries so that she could cook each day. Some days, they invited nearby relatives to join them. She also made enough meals so her father could have some prepared food after they left. But before the cooking began in earnest, Lucille and LaRuth would start the ritual of cleaning Tommy's small house from top to bottom.

Weather permitting — meaning if it wasn't bitterly cold — Lucille would open all the windows to air out the house. She was convinced that fresh air was needed to clear the germs as well as any stale, musty odors that had accumulated since the onset of winter. The two stripped his beds, washed his linen and clothes, dusted practically everything in sight, and wiped down as many of the surfaces as they could.

"You know your mother used to do this kind of cleaning 'fo she got sick," Tommy volunteered.

Lucille smiled and continued pulling off the quilt she was about to take outside to hang on the line. She couldn't remember her mother but liked the idea that she was doing something that reminded her father of her.

There was a lot to do but it never felt like too much to LaRuth or Lucille. LaRuth loved the time with her mother. In addition to being together, Lucille loved that LaRuth seemed to enjoy visiting her Papa Tommy. He loved LaRuth's visits as well, always eagerly anticipating their arrival but never admitting it.

"Y'all know I manage to take care o' myself when y'all ain't here, don't you?" Tommy asked feigning umbrage at the takeover of his house.

"Well, we can just pack up and go on back to Forrest City if we inconveniencin' you," Lucille teased her father.

Smirking at the rise he got out of his daughter, Tommy replied "Ain't nobody said you need to go nowhere. You done come all this way, you might as well stay. 'Sides, I ain't had much time to talk to LaRuth yet."

This particular year, Lucille was especially happy as she had more money to spend on food for her father and to buy apples, oranges, and some hard candies that she could share as Christmas gifts for the younger nearby relatives who otherwise might not get anything at all. She had learned the week before that Mr. Lee had been particularly generous this year.

"Mr. Lee?" Lucille hesitantly questioned her employer after coming to an uncomfortable realization.

"Yes, Lucille?' he answered her inquiring tone with his own.

"I don't believe the amount in my envelope is right," she stated, having looked through the pay envelope that he had given her earlier that day. "There's more in here than I think I'm supposed to have."

"What? Oh yeah." Horton replied. "I forgot to mention that we decided that we hadn't adjusted your pay in a while, so I increased it. Then Della and I added a little something for Christmas and also something extra since we know LaRuth's schooling ain't been cheap. I agreed with Della that we should have helped more."

"Well, I," Lucille started to say before getting a lump in her throat. "I sure do 'pprreciate it, Mr. Lee. I . . . we . . . don't know how to . . ."

"Go on, now," Lee said, with a put-on gruffness. "Don't make a big deal. You earned it. And LaRuth's a good girl."

In addition to the extra money in her pocketbook making this year's holiday visit to her father's a bit more special, Lucille was also joined by her sister Dessie Mae and her half-sister Cardlene. While they both said they were there to help with the cleaning, they spent more time gossiping and catching up. Neither could keep up with Lucille's energy nor share the same satisfaction in the work. That didn't matter to Lucille as she was happy for the company and the chance to spend time with them. Their father seemed to enjoy having his daughters together fussing over him, chattering in the kitchen as they cooked, and filling his small house with laughter.

"Ooo wee, y'all sho' can keep up some racket around here," Tommy said, trying to bait the women as they worked on their various contributions for dinner and caught up on the latest family grapevine. He usually made himself scarce, finding something to do outside or in his little shed. That way, he was close enough that he could keep up with their activity but stay out of the fray and the conversations until he wanted to wade in.

"You want it quiet as a wake at the funeral home?" Dessie Mae offered in retort. "I 'spect you like all this 'racket' but won't give us the satisfaction of sayin' it," she concluded returning to the butter beans she was rinsing, supported by her sisters' echoing "mmm hmms."

Tommy smiled and kept walking out the back door, mission of provoking a response accomplished.

LaRuth enjoyed her time at her grandfather's as well. First and foremost, she loved her Papa Tommy. He was *her* grandfather as she was his only grandchild for many of years. Tommy adored her. She felt it. His countenance never brightened as visibly as when she was around him. As much as he loved his daughters, he loved his granddaughter even more. He made sure to have some kind of treat for her whenever he saw her, be it oranges, peppermints, peanuts, a sweet or a small trinket, whose value was more sentimental than pecuniary. Perhaps he saw in her reserved personality a kindred spirit. Or maybe he was able to pour into her the affection he failed to demonstratively show his own children when they were young given their ages when they went to live with relatives after their mother died. Whatever the motivation, he had clearly communicated to LaRuth that she was special to him. He continued to make her feel that way even as she got older and had to share him as grandfather with her cousins.

The wood stove at Papa Tommy's house reminded LaRuth of her grandmother Effie's house where she had lived with both her mother and father when she was very young, one of her oldest memories. As a small girl, she had loved that Papa Tommy had a little narrow closet off the kitchen that contained a slop jar that saved her from having to use the old outhouse behind his home — especially at night when the experience was a lot scarier since the chances of running into a possum or racoon were greater. Everyone else tended to go outside to the outhouse more often than not but Tommy made sure LaRuth knew she didn't have to if she didn't want to. Fortunately for them all, the jar had a lid so that any smell didn't intrude upon the goings-on in the house. As for the housework, she didn't mind it because she could tell the annual holiday cleaning brought so much pleasure to both her grandfather and her mother.

"LaRuth, how was school this semester?" Cardlene asked.

Just six years her senior and 20 years younger than Lucille, Cardlene was more like an older sister to LaRuth than an aunt.

"It was alright," she replied. "I was ready for Christmas break though. I start some student teacher shadowing for a few days in the spring to get ready for my student teaching assignment next year."

"That's good. I bet you'll like it. Is Dr. Hines still there? I used to love her classes. Her and Dr. Chappell."

"Me, too. Yes, she's still there," answered LaRuth. "I think everybody loves her. She taught some of my friends' parents. She can probably be there for as long as she wants to."

"You haven't gotten it in your head to pledge, have you?" asked Cardlene, changing the subject to sorority life.

"Not me," she replied, wrinkling her nose. "That's a lot of money I don't have. Besides, I don't think I'm their type anyway."

"Type or not, you don't need that extra pressure or anything taking your mind off your studies. If it's like it was when I was there, some of those girls can be really mean. We got to get you graduated, girl! You can always pledge after graduation if you really want to."

Lucille was happy for Cardlene as an example and as a source of moral support for LaRuth. Lucille couldn't offer her daughter any guidance about college herself but she appreciated that Cardlene could and also push her along in ways Lucille didn't know how to do. Lucille would continue to send her prayers, what money she could, and her regular letters encouraging her daughter to pray, "be a good girl," and do her best to make something out of her life.

On their last night together, it was clear that everyone was feeling a little melancholy that the time was coming to an end. Full from dinner and cozy as a result of the stove's heat, they sat in the main room planning to watch a few shows on the used black and white television they had secured for their father a few years before and that he rarely used, preferring the radio instead.

Tommy called to his granddaughter, "Come play me a game of checkers, LaRuth,"

"Yes, sir," she replied, smiling.

As the game progressed, LaRuth tried to divide her attention between the checkers match and *Route 66*, which was beckoning on the TV and that had just come on following *Rawhide*.

"Do you 'member the first time you learnt how to crown a king and what it could do?" Tommy asked with his low, slow voice.

"No, sir," LaRuth responded, trying her best to recall.

"You was yellin' 'King me! King me!' and dancin' a little jig. You almost knocked over the board," he chuckled.

"You couldn't tell her nothing that day," Lucille added, laughing along.

Now convinced that she lacked rhythm and couldn't dance, LaRuth found it amusing that there was a time she wasn't too self-conscious to dance in front of anyone. It pleased her greatly that it was with her mother and grandfather. She hoped to herself that it would be a memory, along with this night, that she might recall one day if she ever became a grandmother.

Following two more moves, LaRuth said "King me," smiling and doing a small jig while seated in her chair, even as she started to suspect that her grandfather had been orchestrating it the whole time.

TWENTY-FOUR

Lee Horton had been around long enough to recognize that today was one of those days that he needed to have a lot of "important things to do" at the store or at the gin — whether it was ginning season or not. His first clue would have been an uptick in Lucille's activity around the house as she had taken the silver serving pieces out of the breakfront, sporting new shines. Also, the china, including the cups and saucers, along with the flatware the Hortons were given when they married, had been placed on the buffet. Additionally, Della's mid-week hair appointment in town was off her usual Friday bi-weekly schedule. The final confirmation for him was the additional sweets that Lucille had baked yesterday without offering him a taste of any of them at dinner last night. All of those developments could mean only one thing: Della was hosting one of her PEO Sisterhood meetings.

"Lucille," he said when Della left the room after finishing breakfast, "You tried to put me in a trick."

"How's that, Mr. Lee?"

Looking around and speaking under his breath, "You didn't warn me to get scarce before this hen party today."

"Oh, I thought you was plannin' to join them this time. Didn't you get your hair did this week?" she said smiling at the thought, turning on the faucet.

Handing her his coffee cup, "I did but I couldn't find the right outfit so I'm gonna pass," he replied, as she continued with the dishes.

"Pass what?" Della inquired, walking back into the kitchen.

"Oh nothing. I've got to get going. Plenty to do at the store today. Have a good meeting."

Lucille could tell that Ms. Della was only half paying attention and had already turned her thoughts to the next item on her mental agenda along with the written to-do list she was holding. Lucille knew that the key to making sure the day was as least stressful as possible for both of them was to address all of her employer's possible concerns proactively before she could obsess over them. Besides, Ms. Della could always find at least one more thing to do, so Lucille needed to have all the other tasks done or at least a plan in place so that she could accommodate the new request.

"I believe just about everything is ready for lunch. I ironed the tablecloth and napkins yesterday and I will lay them out when I finish the dishes. The desserts — the strawberry cake, the lemon cake, and the chess pie — and iced tea are all done, and I'll finish the finger sandwiches after that 'cause the chicken salad is already made. Oh, I forgot about the chocolate pie; it's ready, too. I'll start putting everything in the serving dishes after y'all get into the meeting. I made lemonade just in case someone asks for some. You seemed to like it last time. Anything else you want me to do?"

"Thank you, Lucille. That seems like everything. I do want to put the chocolate pie on that new pedestal stand Bessie gave me if you could take that out. When you get a minute, run down to the store and ask Lee to give you some ice. You can put it in the freezer in case we need some more. Also, iron those linen coasters. I think I want to use them instead of the regular ones." Then, as if to herself, "Did we decide to do those lemon ice-box cookies for the take-aways?"

"Yes, ma'am."

Hosting Ms. Della's chapter of the PEO certainly made for more work, but at this point, Lucille had weathered enough of them to have a system that made the undertaking manageable. As long as the food was tasty and the table was laid out in a way that Ms. Della was pleased, Lucille could navigate the meeting and guests with relative ease and without a lot of mental energy. In spite of the work, she often found them entertaining as well. It had never occurred to her how many seemingly inconsequential issues could cause such vigorous debate. Or how much disagreement there could be about the theme for a spring fundraiser or whether ecru, eggshell or ivory was a more "appropriate" color for invitations than the pale cyan or pink blush that a faction of the group had proposed.

The ladies did spend time on more important business matters as well. Yet, for all their talk about education and scholarships and helping young women, Lucille found it curious that none of them ever thought of asking her if her daughter could use a scholarship — which she certainly could! Instead, most of their comments to her related to more domestic topics.

"Lucille!" exclaimed Margaret Richardson, "You must tell me the secret to your chicken salad! I follow your recipe just like you gave me but mine never comes out as good as yours!"

Of the ladies in the group, Ms. Margaret was certainly one of the nicer ones to Lucille and one of her favorites, though Lucille was aware that some of the women thought Margaret to be "a little flighty" — as whispered to each other — and a little too solicitous of the help. Her brown hair was in a small beehive that highlighted the features of a kind, attractive face. Lucille noticed that her lilac embossed crepe dress had a subtle flower pattern. It wasn't new as Lucille had seen it before but she thought it was a lovely dress. She especially liked the simplicity of the boat-neck collar with the four large diagonal pleats that met in the center to create the fitted bodice and just enough fullness in the skirt to add a slight swing. Although Ms. Margaret was not considered the most fashionable of the crowd, Lucille thought she looked pretty.

"Thank you, Ms. Margaret. I'm sure yours is just as good," Lucille replied, forcing away the pride trying to take over the smile on her face as she filled some of the ladies' iced tea glasses. If she wished any group of folks success with their cooking, it certainly included Ms. Margaret.

"Well, I, for one, can't get enough of these rolls!" added Rose Parsons. "Everything is always so good, Della."

"Why thank you, Rose," answered the group's hostess. Lucille smiled and mused to herself how hungry they would be had they been waiting on all the food Ms. Della had made for the occasion.

"We can tell, Rose," interjected Anne Anderson. "I believe that is your third one already."

"It's a good thing we have you keeping count, Annie," sighed Rose.

"Lucille, how is your daughter doing? Is she still in school over in Pine Bluff?" asked Julia Adams. "What is she studying?" she followed, already a bit absent-minded as she lightly touched her blonde bouffant flip that looked much bigger and more blonde since her last visit.

"Yes, ma'am," answered Lucille. "She's studying to be a teacher."

While she wished her no ill will, Ms. Julia was one of those persons Lucille lost no sleep over whether her recipe attempts ever quite landed. Unlike Ms. Margaret, Julia Adams never came across as sincere and genuine kindness was not her hallmark. Instead, she prided herself on being what she believed to be a recognized fashion-plate. Her new chartreuse — Lucille heard her tell someone the color — day suit was indeed quite fashionable. The fitted two-piece suit featured three-quarter length sleeves and a deep v-cut accented by peak lapels and a white faux blouse that followed the cut of the lapels and with a large white bow at the break that extended several inches on each side of the jacket front. It was indeed a handsome suit though Lucille believed it could have shown better in navy or a darker shade. As it was, the color looked more like something one of the cats threw up the other day, an observation she would never breathe aloud but provided great entertainment in her own mind.

"Well, I think it's wonderful that she's in college. I think more of the colored kids should work harder and go. You must be proud," added Julia. Then continuing without a chance for Lucille to respond, "Rose, pass the broccoli salad, please."

Lucille thought it was funny that Ms. Julia wanted more colored kids to work hard to go to college when everyone knew that her own son had been sent home from Arkansas State over in Jonesboro for not keeping up his studies. Shoot, he could barely drive a tractor straight when plowing their neighboring farm. It took more than a little effort not to "accidentally" drop a bit of salad dressing on the chartreuse suit. Lucille knew she'd have to repent for the thought when she said her prayers later that night.

With lots of additional compliments about the food and a number of guests' threats to Della that they might "steal Lucille away," the sisterhood eventually disbanded amidst plans for their next gathering at the local Methodist church, pleasant good-byes, and little takeaway boxes filled with lemon icebox cookies. Finishing the luncheon dishes and getting everything put away made for a full rest of the afternoon. Fortunately, Ms. Della had told Lucille that she was done for the rest of day — after those tasks were completed — and was free for the next day as she and Lee were driving over to Jonesboro and could eat the lunch leftovers for dinner.

Hallelujah! Her Saturday was hers to do with what she wished and she already knew what that was going to be.

The next morning, Lucille sat with Alexander Winfrey and a few of his sons along the banks of the nearby pond. There were plenty of open spaces among the trees to stand or sit. The Winfreys had brought along a stool for her, as well as one for their father. She was positioned between father and sons, several yards down from Alexander in one direction and several yards from the sons in the other. As it wasn't late morning yet, the sun had not climbed to the top of the sky but there was ample shade once it did. The coolness of the morning was refreshing. Lucille and Alexander were using poles while most everyone else preferred using their rods and reels.

"Watch out there, Lucille," yelled Jessie Winfrey. "Looks like you got a big one on the line!"

Lucille laughed at how Jessie felt the need to tell her what she had already felt and seen. The firm tug followed by the disappearance of the small round red and white bobber on her fishing line meant that she had a fish. The only real question was how big it was. Judging from the pull, it felt like a good-sized one. Sure enough, the crappie that she pulled out was at least three pounds if not larger.

Pole fishing from the banks of the pond was one Lucille's favorite relaxations. She could enjoy it alone just as much as if she were with others like today. She could bait her line with worms without hesitation, although today the Winfreys had gotten minnows and crickets. Jessie and his brothers Aldridge and Elma kept pestering that they were going to get her off the banks and out in their boat but she always resolutely refused. She suspected that they never connected her fear of boats with Walter's drowning and knew their teasing was good-natured.

"I believe this one is gonna cook up good. He might be four or five pounds! Jessie, don't you burn up my fish tonight just 'cause he's bigger than the ones you caught," she goaded.

Their father, Alexander, chuckled from his stool.

Jessie bristled. "You just make sho you bring that coleslaw you supposed to make. I'll handle the frying. 'Sides, when you ever knowed me to burn fish?"

Not to be left out, Aldridge added, "Well you better get busy catching some mo unless you think you gon' feed all o' us with that one fish! You's good but I don't think you can multiply like Jesus."

Answering with a wink and smirk, she stuck out her tongue at Jessie and Aldridge for added emphasis.

After a few hours of fishing at the pond, Lucille returned home to handle a few things before the fish-fry later that evening. Even though this was to be a "day off," she wanted to complete the prep work for the Hortons' Sunday dinner so that she didn't have so much to do when she got back from her own church service the next day. With the chicken seasoned and marinating in the Frigidaire, the beans snapped, the potatoes peeled and a pan of rolls and some summer corn that she had taken out of the freezer to defrost, it wouldn't take much to get tomorrow's meal in order. Of course, she needed to finish the coleslaw she had promised to make for the Winfreys, having chopped the cabbage that morning before joining the fishing party. She also decided to make the cold-oven pound cake from a recipe she had come across and wanted to try. It smelled wonderful as she took it out of the oven. She had already taken the tester that she had made from the oven. A quick sample of the smaller version confirmed that this was a recipe she definitely would make again.

Even though she had told Joe, one of the Winfrey brothers roughly ten years younger than her, that she was going to walk over for the fish fry, he had still come to pick her up and drive her in his truck.

"You just wasting, gas, Joe" she told him. "I could have walked just fine."

"I know you could, but you can let somebody do something for you sometimes," he replied. "You know mama wasn't gon' let us let you walk bringing that food. But if I had knowed you was making a cake, I woulda been over here earlier to sample it for you and make sure it wasn't gon' poison nobody!"

"How you know this one won't?" she retorted.

Lucille loved when she could join the Winfreys for dinner and a fish fry was especially fun. She considered Arrie Winfrey, her husband Alexander, their six boys, some older and some younger than Lucille, family. The couple treated her and LaRuth like they were a daughter and granddaughter. The sons, their wives and their children made for a fun and boisterous gathering whenever they got together. Between a few folding tables and a variety of chairs along with several blankets spread on the ground, there was plenty of room for everyone to eat outside given the mildness of the spring evening.

True to his word, Jessie had fried the fish to perfection. The crappie, bream and catfish were joined by hush puppies, fried potatoes, and Lucille's coleslaw, along with light bread, green tomato relish and pickled okra. The only thing Lucille might have added was sliced tomatoes, but it was too early in the year for fresh tomatoes so the menu really couldn't have been any better she surmised. Wyoming, Joe's wife, had made an apple cobbler — since peaches weren't in season either — to accompany the cakes that her sisters-in-law and Lucille had contributed. In addition, there was plenty of ice-cold water and lemonade to drink. She suspected some of the Winfrey boys had a little moonshine that they were sharing among themselves. She had no interest — having disliked the taste many years before when Walter finally convinced her to take a sip — but she was glad they were enjoying themselves.

"Lucille?" asked Arrie, "How's my girl doin'? She gettin' ready to come out this year, ain't she?"

"Yes ma'am," she answered. "She doin' good. Plannin' to graduate next month — Lord willin'."

"Do she know what she gon' do after that?" Wyoming asked, bumping Lucille's elbow playfully as she sat down nest to her.

"I believe she gon' start teaching, but we ain't sho yet where," nudging Wyoming back with a wink. "She said the school superintendent in Helena was over in Pine Bluff looking for teachers for next year."

"Lord, ain't that somethin'! Our little LaRuth 'bout to be a teacher! You'd think she my daughter I'm so proud," exclaimed Arrie.

"We all are," added Alexander.

"You should be," said Lucille. "Y'all her family and helped raise her, too."

Wyoming giggled. "I forgot to tell you I saw 'Lisbeth in the store yesterday when I was in Forrest City. She actually 'membered who I was and spoke even if I did look like a washer woman."

"Now don't y'all start runnin' down Elizabeth," Arrie interrupted, smiling. "I know she can be a little fussy, but I 'magine she 'bout doin' the best she can with what she have," attempting to nip in the bud the gossip that threatened to ensue.

"Yes, ma'am," replied Lucille. "I reckon she is."

"She may be," Wyoming whispered to Lucille. "But she still a little too sedity if you ask me." Both snickered under their breath and outside the hearing of Arrie.

"Now this is *my* kind of dinner party," Lucille thought to herself. A big family of children was not in the cards for her but she was taking in every minute of her time with the Winfreys and the sounds of their grandchildren running around in the yard. She didn't need to be in all the conversations, often content just to listen and let the fellowship wash over her.

For these few moments, she didn't have to be on alert for her name to be called in case someone needed anything. No "luncheon attendees" to whom she had to be artificially polite. No need to be alert to tensions among feuding guests. No back and forth from her plate in the kitchen to the dining room. No requests to see if there was more rice in the pot. No yells for "Bobo" to come help with a sudden spill or finicky eater.

She could simply be. And relax. And breathe.

With dinner done and dusk silently enveloping the gathering, the ladies made quick work of the dishes outside given the many helping hands. The group sat around listening to music from Joe's radio wafting over the temperate evening breeze as the children's runs around the open yard began to slow down.

Soon the families would start corralling kids and packing up belongings to head to their respective homes.

"Ooo-wee! I'm full as a tick," Wyoming sighed.

Several others smiled and nodded in agreement.

"You heard from Selma and Bam Bam?" Arrie inquired. "Feel like I ain't seen them in a month o' Sundays. They gon' be at church tomorrow?"

"I talked to them last week but not this week. I 'spect they should be there, far as I know," Lucille noted.

"Well, I sure hope Selma is singing. I swear that man sound better than that Sam Cooke if you ask me."

Lucille thought of her cousins and shared Arrie's wish that Selma was doing a solo on Sunday. She loved his voice, too. To her, the best part was that he was so humble about it, genuinely unaware of just how good he sounded.

"You put yo' foot in that cake, Lucille," Alexander offered, another of his rare instances of entering the conversations.

"Thank you, Mr. Alex. You know I'll make you one anytime you want."

"I 'ppreciate that Lucille," Alexander smiled wryly. "But I reckon everyday may be too much — for you and me both."

The entire group joined in the laughter before calling it a night.

TWENTY-FIVE

Route 1 Box 315
Ferrest City Ark
Dear Walter,
 Oh it were so good to see you if it was not two long But you look good and that Case all of you look good Serah were so glad she got to see you all She spent Saturday with me and help feed Mrs Della She say that I am her Neember One Budy Selma Bam Bam Connie all say Hi and fane you to keep going One Mr Russie Call ofter talking to you and he is glad you is planing on Woken up there Give my lane to Juliette and fane her to keep you in Check if not please let me know.
 I lane you moma C.

> *Route 1 Box 315*
> *Forrest City, Ark*
>> *Dear Walter.*
>>> *Oh it were so good to see you if it was not two long. But you look good. And [for] that case all of you look good. Sarah were so glad she got to see you all. She spent Saturday with me and help feed Mrs. Della. She say that I am her Number one Budy. Selma[,] Bam Bam[, and] Connie all say hi and fore you to keep going one. Mr. Russell call after talking to you and he is glad you is planing on worken up there. Give my love to Juliette and fore her to keep you in check. If not pleas let me know.*
>>>> *I love you Moma C.*

I was not prepared for and could not have anticipated the amount of self-examination the journey of chronicling my grandmother's life evoked. I understood that I was wading into waters that required me to deconstruct and analyze her (and other family members') actions and what she must have thought and felt as she lived her life, most of which I came to know well after her death. From the comfort of my current position, now two decades into the third millennium — with a graduate degree, spouse of over thirty years, amazing children, and retirement accounts — I have the luxury of being self-reflective in a way that Mama Ceal most likely could not. I imagine that she did not spend much time engaged in the kind of psychological contemplation that I entertain. To the extent she did, I suppose hers were more existential concerns than esoteric.

For most of her life, from the time she was an adolescent until she retired from her employment as a maid, Mama Ceal had to get up every morning tending to and taking care of the needs of someone else's family so that she could provide financially for her own needs and those of her family. She did so in a hierarchical environment that afforded virtually no status to her as a Black woman while living for the majority of that time — over 42 years — in a roughly 25 foot by 12 foot room that didn't have hot water.

Of all the challenges, heartbreaks, sorrows, indignities, and tests that my grandmother endured, there is something about the fact that she didn't have indoor hot water until she retired at almost 75 and moved in with my mother that remains both poignant and indicting.

The first obvious question of why Mama Ceal didn't have hot water when she moved into the small room attached to the tractor barn and where she lived for over 40 years is easily answered for me. While I don't know it to be true, it's possible that it simply had not occurred to anyone that there was no hot water. The room had been used by a farm hand and there probably had not been a need for hot water in the space. After my grandmother was moved into the room, I suspect the only Hortons who might have spent enough time in her room to see that she didn't have hot water were the children. So it's conceivable that the adults never have had occasion to consider the fact. I want to believe that had the issue been brought to their attention, they might have installed it for her. But I also recognize that it is possible that they might not have wanted to take on that expense. However, from my grandmother's perspective when she moved in, I imagine hot water was not an essential amenity since she didn't have it in the house she was leaving anyway. In addition to electricity, the room had running water, which was a welcome upgrade, itself. Later, when the family installed an indoor toilet and bathtub, she was content to have a hotplate and pot to heat water when she needed it. She continued to heat water for baths, including those for my sister and me, using her hotplate until she moved out of the room in 1990.

I don't know why Mama Ceal never asked that she have hot water in the room. Part of the answer may lie in the idea that she got used to it. In the whole scheme of things, if a lack of hot water was all that was missing, she may have concluded that that shortcoming could be weathered without a lot of difficulty. Because there were limited prospects for alternative work — ones which did not come with room and board — a cost-benefit analysis might result in a practical and reasoned decision to not rock the boat.

As her relatives, we also must have fallen victim to an "it is what it is" mentality as we too never asked the Hortons about providing her with hot water. Or perhaps it was one of those matters better left unspoken since I don't know what we would or could have done had we asked and they declined. In true Southern form, we all were skilled at avoiding conversations that might make anyone uncomfortable. More importantly, it likely would have made Mama Ceal very upset if she learned that we had asked on her behalf, but the fact that we never even discussed it convicts and embarrasses me as well.

I do know that my grandmother loathed the idea of ever asking the Hortons to increase her pay, which probably extended to other kinds of employment-related requests. My mother witnessed firsthand how Mama Ceal refused to entertain her or other relatives' suggestions that she seek a raise. She seemed to feel it was both improper and unappreciative to do so. I also know that Mama

Ceal was especially grateful to work as the Hortons' maid because the job came at a time when she very much needed it for reasons both financial and emotional. Early on, she determined that the Hortons were nice enough people and she could see that she was treated much better than many maids of her time. Over the years, when the sacrifice of sending her daughter to be raised by her sister-cousin became increasingly heartrending and the distance between them seemed to be growing, she came to embrace more and more the feeling that she was a part of the Horton family. She could offer her maternal warmth to their children and fill her lonesomeness with their affection as proxy.

The more upsetting reason that Mama Ceal may have lived without hot water for much of her life could be due to what she thought she was entitled to have. After all, she, too, saw herself as a Black woman in the rural, Jim Crow South. Even if she felt she had a right to such basic comfort, it is also possible that she didn't feel it was proper, given her station, to ask for it. What, then, did she see as her worth?

Considering what my grandmother may have thought of herself forces me to turn this reflective gaze in my direction, bringing to the fore my own quirks and contractions as I highlight hers. How is it that as a confident person who is overall proud of the life that I've been able to build, I am also the person who suffers from imposter syndrome and a tendency to downplay my accomplishments? By the time I was in elementary school, I'd come to accept that I was smart. I had heard enough from teachers, classmates and folks from church, who regularly chose me for leadership roles and the longest Easter and Christmas speeches. Still, the question that took up regular residence in my mind was: Am I really that smart? Most of the time, my answer was "not really."

Similarly though, I try to politely accept — almost always with some self-deprecation — the compliment that I am a good writer Meanwhile, the internal closed captioning that runs in my head like at the bottom of a TV screen is: "Maybe I'm a better editor than a writer and that's what people are responding to." Somewhere along the way, I convinced myself that if I can do it, whatever it is, perhaps it's not that significant of an accomplishment.

It might be tempting to ascribe my tendency for self-deprecation to a performative type of self-modesty. Notwithstanding the fact that such a determination could be true, there are also other dynamics that could be at play.

It is said that during slavery, enslaved parents often tried to minimize or downplay how smart, strong or attractive their children might be. Not only might the attribute make the children more valuable to their owner and, thereby, more vulnerable as targets to be sold to realize that value, but any exceptionalism might also engender resentment among other enslaved persons. There is a belief that Black families still exhibit this custom. Writer Jacquelyn Clemmons notes that "[t]his practice can be seen today in families where Black parents may be proud of their child's achievements and celebrate them at home, but in the presence of mixed company, downplay their children's talents so they aren't seen as a threat."

I recall an instance one summer when my sister and I spent a few weeks during the summer with Momo and attended vacation Bible school at her church. On the evening of the last day, each class hosted a kind of "open house" to showcase to parents and church members our craft projects and also what we had learned that week. I had been assigned the task of explaining a series of pictures capturing well-known stories from the Bible. I don't remember why she happened to be there but Mama Ceal was in attendance that night.

One of the ladies who heard me give my two-minute or less oration said to Mama Ceal, "Oooh, you must be proud. He is so smart. He's going to be a preacher!"

High praise indeed.

Despite the fact that I could tell both that I had done a good job and that Mama Ceal was proud, she replied, "Who, this one? Lord no. He's such a devil." Perhaps the funny — as in odd vs. humorous — thing is I wasn't upset at all that she said it. I knew she didn't really think that I was a devil and her comment put me back on a level with my other Bible-schoolers.

For someone like my grandmother, who was very much a product of her time, it was exponentially more difficult to develop a sense of value and worth when the very structure of society devalued her as poor, as Black, and as a woman even more than it devalues women, minorities, and the poor today. In spite of the advancements and benefits that I have enjoyed and of which my grandmother could only get a brief taste, why do I still have questions about value and self-worth?

I remember once when I was maybe 10 or 11 years old, on a slow Saturday after our cleaning chores had been completed, I asked my mother why we couldn't go shopping. In what I suspect sparked a moment of frustration for my mother, she responded "Why do you think we should go shopping? Don't you know we're poor?" Looking back, I realize that we weren't actually poor even if at that particular time we may have been living paycheck to paycheck and there was not money for frivolities or the latest fad. It was the mid 1970s when both of my parents were employed and our household income was somewhere in the mid $40,000 range, above the median family income for the time. We had just built our home for $39,000, the equivalent of over $200K in today's purchasing power. While my sister and I weren't the most stylish, we had decent clothes and occasionally got items that were popular with our classmates and peers.

But the idea stuck with me: we are poor. As I was already digesting the way society assigns qualitative judgment to those that are deemed poor, I took it to heart as both a depressor but also as a motivator, intensifying the drive and ambition to succeed that I already had. The temptation to use income, material possession, and social standing as arbiters of worth and value is powerful. Even some nearly 50 years later with a household income that puts me well above any definition of poor, there are days that I still wrestle with a concern for being financially secure and that awkward self-consciousness of questioning whether I am enough.

Many years ago, Juliette and I were invited to be guests at a good friend's birthday weekend that his wife was hosting for him in Tulsa. It was the early days of our marriage so being gifted with an all-expense paid trip where all we had to do was show up was a big deal. We otherwise could not have afforded to join the birthday festivities. We had a nice weekend with our friends, sharing experiences as newly married couples and enjoying their months-old baby boy. Per their custom, after church, we went to the country club they belonged to for lunch. As welcome as our hosts made us, it was impossible not to recognize that except for the service staff at the country club, Juliette and I were the only Black people in sight. As we waited in a sitting room with a few other families for our tables to be ready, I observed a young boy playing among the sumptuously upholstered wingback chairs. At one chair, he traced the form of the chair letting his hands fall in and out of the curves as they slid along the leather. At another chair, he put his hands on the back of the chair and then noticed he had inadvertently handled a shoulder bag hanging there. Once he saw the purse, he looked at it and then moved on to the next chair. I chuckled to myself, and later recalled the observation with Juliette. In that moment, particularly mindful of the racial makeup of our location, I imagined myself as a child in that same situation and reacting in a much more nervous and anxious way. Instinctively, I would not have wanted anyone to see me "touching someone's pocketbook" for fear of what recriminations might have ensued. I was struck at the total comfort and lack of concern the little boy had in the situation since he was free of having to worry about what someone might think of him in relation to the purse.

Even though we had not even started the conversation about having children and didn't do so for another couple of years, Juliette replied to me "That's exactly what I want. I want my children to have the freedom to react the same way as that little boy, without the baggage and weight of that kind of apprehension you felt. I want them to know that they have the right to be in any environment they find themselves in." Sure enough, we raised (mostly she) our "country club" children. Our inside baseball definition of "country club" though in no way resembles what the term ordinarily connotes or brings to mind. Instead, we use it in that context to reference someone who has a strong sense of self and who feels they are entitled to take up space wherever they are, not because of any amount of money or education or accomplishment they have attained, but because they are a human being worthy of the dignity, respect, courtesy and consideration due every human being. Someone who appreciates and walks in their inherent worth of self.

Growing up . . . living . . . being Black in this country can breed a certain level of self-questioning and doubt. Because of that, I have a deep appreciation, respect, and awe for both forebearers and contemporaries who get past the "noise" and demonstrate the strength, courage, and grit to be the "first" or the "only" or the 63,457th who have been willing to strike new paths, kick open doors, or simply take up space. I have a similar awe for my children, who would make my grandmother beam with more pride than she could measure and an endless stream of tears.

Perhaps it's human nature that confidence and self-doubt can co-exist in the same space. Maybe it isn't unusual to have a strong sense of self and yet also question your worth. I don't think that Mama Ceal spent much time contemplating these debates as I have. Yet, whether those concepts are commonplace or not, I find it particularly reassuring knowing that even if my own children find themselves wrestling with these same questions, they will do so in a way that gives much less effect to whether they are Black or poor or queer. Even with the many "isms" our country and world continue to grapple with, and despite the surge of intolerant, ideological campaigns against those "other people," the milieu is at least somewhat less oppressive and more accepting than the world my grandmother navigated. Mama Ceal's "country club" great grandchildren have the composure and self-confidence to speak up to address whatever their "hot water" issues may be because they know they are worth it and have a right to do so. Mama Ceal would agree.

TWENTY-SIX

As she rubbed her ear, LaRuth wondered whether there was any truth to the old wives' tale that someone must have been talking about her at that moment. Laughing, she figured if there was, it had to have been her mother telling someone else about her graduation from college. Given the number of times that Lucille had mentioned the upcoming commencement in her letters, LaRuth could tell that her mother's eagerness was palpable. While she was excited herself — and a little nervous — since she didn't know for sure yet that everything was in place for her to graduate, LaRuth knew that whatever emotion she felt didn't compare to her mother's anticipation. Lord willing, in a few months, she would be able to give her mother this long-held dream.

Perhaps it was the proximity of graduation, along with the realization that it was not guaranteed that had her in such a pensive mood. Almost four years ago, the idea of graduation was so far away that she couldn't let herself even imagine it. As much as she wanted to be away from home, she was also nervous about how she was going to fit in and whether she would have any friends. She had tried to be brave for her family that day they dropped her off but inside she was a bag of nerves. Liz, her closest confidante and pal up to that point, had made the decision — or rather it was made for her by her family's finances — not to go to college. She had moved to Indianapolis to live with an older sister and pursue the promise of a job. Making it through college without Liz seemed like a superhuman task that she knew she had to tackle but also one she hadn't expected to be particularly enjoyable.

Her first couple of days only underscored her trepidation. The system of assigning roommates by last name had not mistreated her the way some had felt, but neither had it done her any great favors. She watched how some housing pairs seemed made for each other as immediate friendships were formed. By partial contrast, she and the young woman with whom she shared a freshman room were not exactly at the opposite end of the spectrum. They were civil enough and held no animosity toward each other, but great friends they were not destined to be. Still, their dormitory, Lewis Hall, in the end, did prove to be the source of her most valued college relationships.

Still pondering graduation while walking into the Student Union building, she waved at her friend Carrol across the lobby. Each on separate missions, neither interrupted her course as they knew they could catch up later at dinner or in the dorm. Carrol Tillman was from Marianna, a small hamlet not that far from Forrest City. Despite the proximity of their hometowns, the insular, close-knit nature of the regional Black community, and the fact that their families knew many of the same people, somehow, they hadn't met until matriculating at AM&N.

Sitting down next to LaRuth in one of their early classes, Carrol asked, "Aren't you from Forrest City?"

On the surface, many might have seen theirs as an unlikely friendship — and LaRuth probably would have agreed with them. Carrol was more self-assured and outgoing; she chatted easily with anyone. She also was interested in pledging Alpha Kappa Alpha, a Black sorority, even if it had to wait until after she graduated and had the money to do it. She wasn't the most obvious choice of pals for the more reserved LaRuth. Yet, they both shared a number of characteristics, including humble backgrounds, unassuming demeanors, keen eyes for observing people, and an uncanny ability to hear all manner of conversations taking place around them without giving the slightest indication that they were even listening. They also shared the same business administration major, so they found themselves in many of the same classes after freshman year.

Catching herself smiling, she realized that her dread of completing college completely without friends was a bit overblown, but the fact that her initial concern was so wrong pleased and amazed her. In one of her prouder — and braver — moments, it was LaRuth who had initiated her friendship with Billie Pryor when she invited her to walk to the cafeteria for dinner one evening during their first week on campus. Having seen her a few times after they had moved in, LaRuth noticed that Billie seemed a little down that day. Before she thought about it too much and talked herself out of it, LaRuth did what she felt she would have wanted someone to do had she been in a similar mood.

"Thanks for asking me to come to dinner with you," Billie smiled as they walked into the cafeteria.

"No problem. You're welcome. You doing okay?"

"I guess I'm okay," replied Billie. "I didn't expect to be homesick so soon."

"I know what you mean. I was excited to be away from home and away from all the rules but I do miss it. I even miss my aunt. Lord knows I sure didn't expect that," LaRuth added laughing.

Recognizing a kindred spirit during that first exchange, they each had taken to the other right away. To have someone like Billie express such immediate and unreserved fondness was heartening for LaRuth and bolstered her self-confidence. The foundation for a lifelong friendship had been laid. Neither of them could have conceived that when Billie introduced her Uncle Marvin to LaRuth years later, she was setting the stage for them to ultimately marry one day.

Then there was Grace.

"You know, girl, I thought you might be too serious for me. You're so quiet and always studying so much that I felt silly around you" laughed Grace one evening as they played Bid Whist. "You're actually fun!" she exclaimed in mock disbelief. "And you can play some cards! I'm gon' make sure we are partners all the time."

Grace Wilbert, who hailed from El Dorado, was gregarious and loved to laugh — the life and energy of the gathering whenever the friend group was together. One evening, Carrol had made popcorn on the small hotplate in her room and convinced some of the girls to join a card party in the dorm lounge. LaRuth and Grace did not already have partners for the card game and were paired up by Carrol. LaRuth loved Grace's sincerity and exuberance. She reminded LaRuth of her mother in some ways. Although they had known each other from a distance and spoken in passing, it wasn't until that evening that they interacted closely enough to plant the seeds of friendship. LaRuth liked that she never had to wonder what Grace was thinking because she was definitely going to let you know.

Grace also had a boyfriend, a nice guy named George Charles who was on the football team. Although he transferred to Southern University after their first year, LaRuth, Billie, and Carrol admired and looked up to George like a protective big brother. Where you saw George, you usually saw Grace and vice versa. Several of her friends had teased her about how she was going to make it without George after he transferred. Of course, Grace always said in response that the question they should be asking is how was George going to make it without her.

"Why are we all sitting up here still hungry and looking pitiful?" fumed

Grace one evening in the fall of their sophomore year.

"Because they were serving mystery meat tonight," huffed Carrol.

"No. I mean why are we not doing something about it?" answered Grace.

Carrol sucked her teeth. "Just what do you propose we do about it, Miss Wilbert?"

"Well, between the four of us, we ought to have enough money to go get something across the street," Grace answered, referring to the Lion's Den, a small comfort food joint across from the college where, if they had money, they could find something to satisfy in-between-meal cravings or, as in this case, make up for a particularly bad dining experience in the cafeteria. On that evening, they pooled their resources and ensured that each of them could have a filling if not gourmet meal — a bowl of beans and cornbread.

With the potential of graduation looming, LaRuth was prone to reliving many of the memories that she had shared with her friends. Among those memories, of course, was Homecoming. Characterizing the annual Homecoming activities as part cultural celebration, part alumni reunion, part community festival, part Greek fraternity and sorority step-show, part band competition, all organized around a football game only somewhat captured the spectacle the event was for the students. While Homecoming was always an enjoyable phenomenon each year, she knew without question that being able to experience it with her three girlfriends couldn't be matched.

"Isn't Grace coming to the parade?" LaRuth asked Billie as they walked among the students trekking the mile and a half to downtown Pine Bluff for the Homecoming parade.

"Girl," replied Billie, rolling her eyes, "You know Grace is still sleep. We better hope that she's up by the time we get back so we aren't late for the game."

"You're right," chuckled LaRuth. "But you know she's going to be mad she missed the bands."

"Well, at least she might see the half-time show. But what you want to bet she won't miss the dance though?" teased Billie.

Of course, Grace did not miss the dance.

Continuing on her mission of checking her mailbox in the Student Union, LaRuth couldn't think of any of her friends or classmates who received mail as regularly as she did. Her mother was nothing if not faithful in sending letters, usually weekly. LaRuth was such a regular visitor at the campus post office that the staff and students who worked the mailboxes had come to know her and her mother's letter schedule. They often asked how her mother was doing or when she was going home to see her.

Along with a notice about an upcoming student recital and one about a speaker sponsored by Alpha Phi Alpha Fraternity, sure enough, there was one small envelope in her box with the familiar handwriting and Forrest City return address even though it had originated in Newcastle. Occasionally, she tried to make time to write a letter back but more often than not she managed to get caught up in something else. Fortunately, her mother knew that she wasn't much of a letter writer. In fact, Lucille never expected replies and was pleasantly surprised when the occasional missive found its way to the mailbox.

"Tell your mother I'm still waiting on my letter," Mrs. Taylor teased LaRuth when she saw her pass the service window.

"Yes, ma'am," LaRuth smiled, pausing to wave to the warm-faced woman who reminded her of a brown Mrs. Santa Clause. She knew that had she actually delivered this message to her mother, Mrs. Taylor would have her own letter the next week. She loved that her mother never met a stranger and shared her geniality without reservation. LaRuth liked to think that her mother's sociability and openess made up for her own more cautious friendliness.

Fortunately, that cautiousness hadn't impeded her most valued relationships. As an only child, she couldn't say for sure what having sisters was like. But she was grateful she had had the chance to share her college experience with her three closest friends, akin to sisters as far as she was concerned.

Opening the envelope that she had just retrieved from her mail slot and unfolding the notepad-sized piece of paper inside, Lucille's warmth enfolded LaRuth as she began to read the words. She could hear her mother's voice.

Dear LaRuth,
Just few lines to let you here from me. This leve me ok. Thank the Lord. Hope you are two. I went to church and Selmer and Bam Bam say tell you they is proud of you. You know that make me feel good. They say they is praying for you two. You must be bussie with school. I am excited about commen fore gradashun. You be a good girl. And dont fore get to pray.
Love Moma

"Yes, that confirms it," LaRuth thought to herself. Her mother was definitely telling someone else about graduation when her ear had itched. She imagined all of Newcastle must know at this point. "God help me if I don't graduate," she gulped under her breath.

How was it that the early weeks of uncertainty, the periods of occasional loneliness, and the moments of absolute joy, excitement and discovery had morphed into four years that were about to come to an end? She remembered when Aunt Elizabeth had gone to the AM&N Vesper Choir concert at a church in Forrest City as part of their tour a couple of years ago. She imagined Aunt Elizabeth showing up with a cake and some containers of frozen greens and peas trying to find a choir member in her dorm who was willing to bring the food back to her "daughter." LaRuth got major points when she shared her largess with her friends. LaRuth could tell Aunt Elizabeth felt good when LaRuth told her how much she and her friends enjoyed it.

While many students complained of the mandatory attendance at Vespers Service every Sunday evening, she found the tradition grounding. The services reminded her of going to church at home, but fortunately weren't as long. She appreciated having the regular opportunity to quiet her mind and center herself.

She thought back to meeting her first real boyfriend, Harold Vanhoose, a kindhearted, earnest young man from Tuscaloosa, Alabama, who was on the football team. He had stopped to speak to her one evening after the team made its nightly trek past the women's dorm and as she and a few other young ladies were sitting on the benches outside chatting.

Walking LaRuth home after a weekend dance, Harold noted, "I think it's funny that you couldn't care less that I'm on the football team."

"Why is that? If you needed more of an admirer, you could have had one of those girls batting her eyes and trying to snag a football player. You approached me, remember?"

"I remember. And, for the record, I wasn't complaining. The fact that you didn't seem to care is exactly why I stopped to talk to you. Some of those fangirls didn't have much respect for themselves. You did. Plus, I had seen you around campus. You seemed serious about your work."

"So, you wanted a boring nerdy girl who was grateful to have you?" laughed LaRuth.

"I wanted a nice girl who I wouldn't mind my mother meeting."

"Ahhh. Good answer. Well, you're not so bad yourself but you got a ways to go before meeting my mother," she replied giggling.

Harold responded with a hip bump to hers as they made their way to the dorm.

She also remembered some of the bumps in the road during her college career. While she had surely enjoyed her time at AM&N, or "State College" as it was sometimes known, her time had not been a completely easy, carefree four years by any means. Navigating the post-secondary landscape can be a challenge for anyone, but when you add the turbulence of the late 1950s through the mid-1960s, the mission took on a whole new significance in a context fraught with risk. As LaRuth spent this period of her life spreading her wings and pushing boundaries, the country too experienced its own testing of societal limits and proscriptions that forever impacted its future. The mounting frustration and impatience among Black people (and their allies) and the resulting demonstrations and protests that were emblematic of the Civil Rights Movement were engulfing the country, including the small town of Pine Bluff, Arkansas, and its flagship AM&N.

In 1958, the year before she entered college, the school president Lawrence A. Davis, Sr. drew the ire of Arkansas Governor Orval Faubus and the state legislature after he invited a young civil rights leader, Rev. Martin Luther King, Jr. to serve as the graduation speaker. When Davis later appeared before the legislature in support of the school's budget request, he was publicly criticized and berated for "double-crossing" the state officials by having King speak. Not only did the legislators remind the president of their ultimate control of the college's fate as holders of the purse strings, they reduced some of the institution's funding to underscore the message. One of the ways the classes who entered AM&N after such a cut, including LaRuth's, felt the effects of that funding change was in the poorer quality of the previously beloved food service in the cafeteria — a service that had been highly regarded by the students. The fallout of that skirmish lasted into LaRuth's time on campus when Governor Faubus later supported efforts to replace Davis as president with someone more palatable to him and the legislature, a move that was met with a fierce response from the college community and Pine Bluff's Black population.

"Well, the Student Government officers have said that everybody needs to either drop some of their classes or at least not go so that we send a message to Faubus that they can't push Prexy around like that just because he let Rev. King come speak," remarked Carrol as several residents of Lewis Hall considered how to respond to the efforts to oust the president.

"Fay Helen said that the coaches told the football players that they better not drop any classes but they didn't say they couldn't miss class," replied Grace.

"But I don't understand what dropping a class is going to do," added Billie. "Can you get back in the class if you drop it? Shoot! My father will kill me if I drop a class we already paid for."

"LaRuth?" queried Grace, "What are you gon' do?"

All eyes turned to LaRuth since she had not otherwise been participating in the conversation, seemingly consumed in her Business Law text book.

"What they're trying to do to the president is wrong. But I can't see dropping a class. Between my mother and my aunt, I wouldn't have an inch of skin left if they realized I couldn't graduate because I dropped a class."

"So you not gon' do it?" Grace blurted out.

"But," LaRuth continued as though there had been no interruption, "If enough of us miss classes and they can't teach them — which I believe is the point — that might be enough to make the Governor and those state folks think again and leave Prexy alone. Besides, we can still make up the time and take our exams. Plus, our families won't have any reason to know. If they do find out, it won't matter that much since we haven't hurt our studies."

LaRuth and her friends joined the already committed and some of the previous waverers in heeding the rallying call of the student government leaders to skip their classes in support of their beloved president. The students' efforts were rewarded. The state officials who had floated the idea of getting rid of Davis dropped the scheme when they realized that the consequences of the backlash were far worse than putting up with an otherwise seemingly reasonable college administrator in spite of his perceived lapse in judgment.

That, however, was not the only conflict to impact the small campus during LaRuth's time as a student. In fact, it was minor compared to what was to come. In early 1963, the year she was scheduled to graduate, AM&N students and town residents witnessed another expression of the growing social and racial tension and unrest. On February 1, students from the college attempted to integrate the F. W. Woolworth lunch counter in downtown Pine Bluff. When the contingent asked for service that day, the waitress refused and turned off the lights. The 13 students sat at the counter and stood nearby for three hours until it was time for the store to close. They left but returned day after day with more and more students and were met with the same response on the part of Woolworth employees — ignoring the contingency and turning off the lights at the lunch counter. Having seen other protests play out around the country, and more motivated by his desire to safeguard his store than any concern for the protestors, the manager in Pine Bluff had chosen a path that involved the least risk to property.

The student protestors and the larger community were lucky that somehow the AM&N students' acts of civil disobedience weren't met with more violent reactions. Three years earlier to the day, four students at North Carolina Agricultural and Technical State University had begun a sit-in that lasted for roughly five months and grew from the initial four protestors to over a thousand, including students from nearby Bennett College, a historically Black women's college, and Dudley High School, a segregated Black high school. The students were taunted and heckled by Woolworth customers as well as members of the local KKK. Fortunately, no one was injured.

Closer to home in neighboring Louisiana, just over a year before the Pine Bluff conflict, 23 students at another historically Black college, Southern University in Baton Rouge, had been arrested for picketing in front of segregated stores. The over 1,500 students who responded by protesting in front of the jail where the arrestees were being held faced a harsher response: many were teargassed, set upon by dogs, chased by police, beaten with nightsticks, and ultimately arrested. Grace's boyfriend, Charles, who had transferred to Southern at that point, was among those arrested, though he wasn't beaten. Ultimately, he was released since the jail was already full by the time his group was picked up and the police couldn't hold all of the students they had detained.

News of the Pine Bluff protest activities gained attention across the city and state. President Davis again faced pressure from members of the Arkansas State Legislature, this time to put his foot down and bring the disruptive actions on the part of his students to an end. LaRuth, like other students and staff, as well as members of the larger Black community, had heard the rumors that Davis supposedly had met privately with the students, expressing his moral support for their efforts. Publicly, though, with no other option available to him if he wanted to avoid the potential closure of the college, Davis was quoted in an open letter published in the local Pine Bluff paper advising any students participating in the demonstrations to withdraw from AM&N. Those who did not, he warned, would be expelled.

"I see you got one of those flyers under your door, too," Billie said to LaRuth as they sat around one of the tables in the study lounge of the dorm with Grace and Carrol. The four friends found themselves once again debating as they had a couple of years before their role in the events of the day.

"Mmm hmm," LaRuth mumbled.

"Those two girls from Little Rock down the hall from me already signed up to join the protest," added Carrol.

"My friend Margaret said she doesn't believe Prexy will expel anybody. That he just said that to please the White folks," Grace chimed in. "LaRuth?" queried Grace. "LaRuth!"

"Huh? What?" she answered. "I'm sorry. What did you say?"

"Where is your mind, girl? You off in space somewhere?" chided Carrol. "We're talking about the sit-in. We need to figure out what we are going to do. I say we can't just let other folks fight our battles all the time," she continued. "Where would we be if everybody only thought of themselves? Shoot, we might not even have a college to go to if folks didn't step up and demand it!"

"You right," replied LaRuth. "But right now, I don't know."

What LaRuth hadn't shared with her friends was that she had had a similar conversation with her friend Samuel a few days earlier. Samuel Williams was a senior business major from West Memphis. Other than their separate physical education courses, Samuel and LaRuth had been in most of the same classes since their sophomore year. While they had their own sets of friends, the two had become close themselves and had spent many afternoons engaging in all kinds of discussion, from the deep to the silly and sharing tips for homework assignments, stories about their families, and dreams for the future.

"LaRuth, I really feel like we need to support the sit-in," said Samuel as they left a business economics class after putting on their coats. "I just don't know how I can sit by and let those guys take on the whole load for all of us."

"Yeah, I get it, but I'm torn. On the one hand, it ticks me off how we are treated," she continued as they made their way across the yard bundled warmly against the February cold. "Even when I might have a little extra spending money, I hardly ever go downtown to the stores anymore because I can't stand to see how those little ladies who look like my mama or my aunts can't try on the clothes they want to buy and get sneered at when they are trying to spend their money that is just as green and worth just as much as White folks' money."

As they walked and continued the conversation, LaRuth couldn't help being distracted as they passed the campus bell tower. She had always loved the tradition of its regular chimes throughout the day. However, it was the tower's solid brick structure that stood unapologetic in the center of campus as a symbol of the strength and integrity of the institution that was most appealing to her. The tower was a reminder to LaRuth that there was strength in her, a strength that meant she could weather whatever challenges she faced in college. More than once, she had looked to the iconic edifice for inspiration and encouragement during her years at AM&N.

Making herself return to the conversation with Samuel, she continued, "And I hate being stared at and followed around like I'm about to steal something whenever I go in a store."

"Exactly!" replied Samuel. "It's disrespectful. It's humiliating. Hell, it just ain't right! I've decided I'm going to join the sit-in. I don't know a whole lot of other people to ask but I want you to really think about doing it, too."

"But what about the chance we might get expelled?"

"I think the president had to say that. You know he's all for civil rights. He brought Dr. King here, remember? But even if it is a possibility, what we fighting for is way bigger than getting expelled."

"Yeah, it is. But that's not the only thing I got to think about. I got my mama and my aunt and a whole lot of other folks expecting me to graduate. It just ain't that simple."

"Look, don't answer right now, but promise me you'll think about it?"

"Alright," she sighed. "I'll think about it. I will. But I can't make no promises."

The talk with Samuel had upset her — not because he had asked but because she found herself actually considering whether she might join the protests. She had been preoccupied by Samuel's request ever since.

In addition to wondering what her mother would say, complicating matters for LaRuth was the voice of Aunt Elizabeth in her head as well.

"Rabble rousers who don't have any home-training," she could hear Elizabeth saying and imagined her lack of sympathy for the protestors. While Aunt Elizabeth could acknowledge the unfairness Black people faced, LaRuth imagined her aunt would surely feel that demonstrating and protesting was not the way to demonstrate to White folks that you were a respectable Negro who merited their regard. LaRuth knew that Elizabeth would have been furious to know she had joined the class walk-out a few years earlier. Lord only knows how much more enraged she would be if LaRuth was expelled for protesting — at a Woolworth lunch counter where the food wasn't even that good anyway!

"Well, *I* know," asserted Grace, pulling LaRuth back to the conversation at hand. "Y'all saw those Klan on the news in Greensboro. I told you how those crackers set them dogs on George and those other students at Southern when they were marching outside the jail. Half of 'em got beat up by the police. And you know the police here ain't no better. Them kids were lucky they didn't get lynched."

"I know that's right," Billie replied. "I'm scared of the police and my folks. I don't think I can do it either. Lord, Jesus."

LaRuth had agreed to meet Samuel at the Lion's Den to talk more about his proposition the following day. He arrived early and ordered a snack of a grilled cheese sandwich for them to share. LaRuth wished that she could lose herself in the maroon and silver pattern of the Formica table where they were sitting. She knew that continuing to focus on the smell of the neckbones and collards that were advertised as the day's special was only delaying the inevitable.

"I couldn't stop thinking about what you said," LaRuth stated after thanking him for the sandwich. "I know we got to have folks stand up for us and for our people."

"But," interjected Samuel, "I can hear it coming," anticipating what her demeanor was already telling him.

"But this time, it ain't gon' be me. I don't know what my mama might say about the sit-in — and she very well may support it. But what I *do* know is that she expects me to graduate. And I can't do that if I'm expelled. I know y'all don't think anybody is going to get expelled but nobody knows for sure."

"I understand," replied Samuel, begrudgingly finishing the last bite of his portion of the sandwich.

"I know you think you do but what I really need you to understand is that graduating from college has been Mama's biggest dream for me since I was little, since before my daddy died. I can't put that at risk — no matter how much I think it's right," she stated, sounding defeated. "I'll be praying for all of y'all — especially, you Samuel, if you decide to do it — but I just can't. Come hell or high water, I have to graduate for my mother."

In spite of President Davis's warnings, Samuel and several other students joined the protest. The sit-ins continued, lasting a total of 28 days. When the student demonstrators arrived at Woolworth's on that last day, they found that the store had ended lunch service completely, removing the stools and covering the entire counter. While the students had not achieved their goal of integration, they sent a strong message that the force of the Civil Rights Movement was present and active in Pine Bluff. True to the public statement, President Davis suspended and then expelled 15 students, including Samuel, the human sacrifices to his goal of preserving his institution's existence.

Making her way back to the dorm after leaving the Student Union building, LaRuth had enough time to get in some reading before she'd join the girls for dinner. She shuddered as she thought about how close she came to being one of the students expelled for participating in the sit-in. She had justified her decision not to join Samuel based on what she needed to do for her mother, but the fact was she wanted the accomplishment of graduating from college as much as or maybe even more than her mother did. She *needed* to graduate for herself. Both mother and daughter had given up a lot for that goal. Had they sacrificed too much? She wasn't sure, but was starting to see that she was perhaps more like her mother than she had recognized. She didn't know what the sacrifices might be, but she knew that she couldn't say what she would or wouldn't be willing to do when considering college for the children she hoped to have one day.

For now, marriage and children and who knows what else were events far away in her distant future, all new experiences in new phases of life that were to come — but not before she secured for her mother and for herself the one thing they had dreamed of for so long.

TWENTY-SEVEN

Lucille was glad that she had followed her first mind and decided to sit on the Hortons' porch to shell the bushel of purple hull peas that the Winfreys had shared with her, enough that she could cook some this week and put some in the freezer. She was already tasting the hot water cornbread she would make to go with them. The chow chow she had put up last year would add a nice touch to the meal.

The hottest part of summer was over and the cool of the coming fall was several weeks away. It was still warm but not roasting like the prior week — a holdover from the scorching days of August. But today was just mild enough that she preferred being outside rather than in the air-conditioned kitchen. While she liked the comfort of the air conditioner on really hot days, sometimes the cool felt too artificial. Today she wanted to feel the warmth of the weather and recall the days before air conditioners. She was happy to enjoy the fresh air that blew through the screened porch. The screening kept the annoying flies from bothering her and also stopped any pesky mosquitoes as well though it was too early in the day for them to be stirring.

Out of the blue, with the sun beaming as bright as any summer day, a light rain started, neither challenging the other so much as coexisting. Lucille thought to herself: "The Devil is beating his wife."

Shelling peas was a meditative task for Lucille; she could think on any number of things or nothing at all as she hummed to herself while she worked. Grabbing a handful of pea pods in her left hand, she used the nail and tip of her right thumb to open and then pushed her finger from one end of the pod to the other to dislodge the kidney-shaped seeds. On this pleasant mid-September afternoon, the sound of the peas plopping into her metal bowl and hitting its sides reminded her of heavy rain drops hitting a tin roof at the beginning of a spring shower. The rote motion of releasing the creamy and slightly green tinted peas from their long purplish encasements freed her mind to count her blessings, which she imagined numbered as many as the orbs sitting in her lap. She could almost hear last Sunday's hymn from church — *It Is Well With My Soul* — playing alongside her thoughts.

Despite the difficulties and heartaches she had experienced, Lucille realized that she was blessed. It hurt that she couldn't remember her mother, but her father was a good man and had tried to do right by her and the family. Papa Ed and Mama Liza, God rest their souls, had been so loving and kind; they had given her as good of a childhood as she figured she had a right to expect. Certainly, she would have loved to have shared a long life with Walter and she would never fully get over his drowning. But, oh, what a beautiful time they had together — even if it was short and they were dirt poor, barely able to get by. She couldn't picture her life not having met him or growing to love him . . . or becoming his wife. It was strange, she thought, how being grateful and counting her blessings also brought a little sadness with the gratitude.

Of course, there was LaRuth. Thank the Lord that He gave her that girl. Living for her daughter was the main thing that kept her going after Walter's death. It had been hard sending her to live with Owen and Elizabeth and it was even harder after she lost Walter. The worst part was that it meant their times together were so limited — especially during the very periods a child should be with her mother. She saw that even more clearly now having watched John and Carl grow up right there under her feet. A pang of melancholy over her lost moments had taken a seat right next to the lump of grief she held for her deceased husband. Yes, this was the one thing that still gnawed at her and distracted from her ability to be completely grateful: the plaguing ache of the time she had missed with LaRuth.

The separation they experienced had led to a distance between her and LaRuth, a distance that Lucille didn't know how to bridge. She never questioned whether her daughter loved her. That she could feel in her heart and she could see in LaRuth's eyes. But there was also a way that they couldn't talk easy with each other the way that they seemed to with other people. There was a strain that hung in the air sometimes when they were together. She wondered whether her daughter could ever fully understand or get over being sent to live with her aunt and uncle. For that matter, Lucille wondered whether she herself could get over it. However, that was now water under the bridge and the reason for the separation — the crazy dream of a sharecropper and washer woman —

had been realized: LaRuth had graduated from college. Maybe one day they all might be able to say that it was worth the cost. She whispered a prayer that God forgive her if she seemed ungrateful indulging these feelings.

Enough of that she resolved. There was plenty to be thankful for.

Lucille didn't fully understand what LaRuth's job after college was since it wasn't teaching as she had planned. But it was in an office and LaRuth was using what she had learned in school to do it. Her college graduate was not washing other folks' clothes or chopping someone else's cotton or cleaning anyone's house but her own. That was indeed a blessing.

While she had no wish to die an early death, Lucille felt that if the good Lord called her home that day, she could go a content woman. What did the future hold? She didn't know, but she dared not ask God for more. All in all, she had enjoyed a good life, rich beyond her deserving. She was grateful for this moment to be grateful.

Lucille looked down at how the hulls were staining her fingertips a slight plum color. She raised her hands from the bowl, turning them over, and realized that LaRuth's hands looked like hers, maybe less callused and with fewer needle pricks, but the same, nonetheless. She smiled.

She decided to save some of the hulls and boil them down to make purple hull pea jelly. She would share some with Dessie Mae and LaRuth. She'd even give some to Elizabeth.

After graduation, without an immediate teaching offer, LaRuth accepted a position as a secretary with a local office of the state Cooperative Extension Service located in Augusta, Arkansas, a small town in Central Arkansas, about an hour's drive from Forrest City and two hours from Pine Bluff where she had gone to school. An agency of the U.S. Department of Agriculture, the Cooperative Extension Service's mission was to improve the lives of people in predominantly rural communities. Extension service employees shared research-based knowledge and skills to support efficient farming, promote healthy lifestyles, and enhance teacher quality in primary and secondary schools, among other objectives. LaRuth liked that the agency was helping people like her mother and her family. Additionally, she knew a few folks from college who were also working in Augusta so the move there was not as bad as if she hadn't known anyone at all. Plus, she was close enough to Forrest City that she could return home to visit her mother and other family about once a month or so.

Another added benefit for LaRuth was that several of her acquaintances and colleagues in Augusta made regular weekend trips to Pine Bluff, making it easy for her to visit her college friend Billie, who was working and living there. Sometimes, the two attended a football game at AM&N or dropped by a house party thrown by friends. Other times they just hung out together, catching up on the latest gossip regarding classmates and commiserating about how hard it was to go to work every day instead of leading the life of a college student. Of their college crew, Billie and LaRuth were able to maintain the most consistent contact since everyone else had gone farther away. Seeing each other regularly helped ease their transition into "real" adulthood. LaRuth was also glad that she could be a source of support to Billie when her father died within a few months of their graduation. She traveled to Billie's hometown of Nashville for the funeral and later offered her a safe space to grieve.

Then, there was the weekend that started out like any of her other visits to see Billie but that would become a turning point in her life. She arrived on Friday evening to find that Billie had some family over.

"LaRuth," said Billie, "This is my Uncle Marvin. I introduced you to him at the funeral."

"Yes, nice to see you, again," LaRuth nodded politely. She had not realized that anyone else was joining them for the basketball game weekend they had planned but apparently Billie's uncle would be.

"Nice to see you as well. I hear this is supposed to be a good game tomorrow. Prairie View is giving everybody a run for their money this year," responded Marvin.

By Sunday, they, including Marvin and a couple of other friends, had spent time together at the game, a group dinner on Saturday night, and a visit to Billie's church. Among other things, LaRuth had learned that Marvin, who also lived in Pine Bluff, was recently divorced. Her initial uncertainty whether he was showing an unusual interest in her was confirmed when Billie shared her observation as LaRuth was leaving to go back to Augusta, "I think he likes you."

Marvin had not swept her off her feet, but he had been pleasant enough and his sense of humor kept her and Billie laughing throughout the weekend. She didn't think much else of Billie's comment until the next week when she got a call from Marvin asking if he could come visit her in Augusta. *Why not? What have I got to lose?* she thought to herself.

Within the span of a few months, between his "showing up" whenever she went to see Billie, his visits to Augusta, and several invitations to accompany him to family cookouts and gatherings in Little Rock, they had become "an item."

By the fall of 1964, it was Billie who was called on to provide support to LaRuth as they tackled another of life's unexpected, watershed moments.

Billie could tell something was wrong the moment LaRuth walked into the house. The smile from LaRuth's firmly pressed lips quickly gave way as she said goodbye to the people she had ridden with and closed the door.

"What's wrong?" Billie questioned, moving quickly to her friend. "You look a mess."

"Billie," LaRuth confided to her friend, wiping away tears that had started to flow and seemingly stuck in the spot where she had stopped in the small living room. "I'm pregnant."

"Oh, honey," Billie answered, trying to be consoling. She put her arm around LaRuth and moved them both to the sofa. In all the years that they had known each other, Billie had never seen LaRuth so distraught. She could feel LaRuth spiraling even as they sat momentarily silent, absorbing the disclosure that changed everything.

"Never mind that I'm not married. That's plenty bad enough. But now Marvin tells me that his divorce," she punctuated with air quotes, "is not final yet! Do you think that Negro could have thought to tell me that before now? What am I gon' do?" she continued, barely pausing to breathe. "Oh Lord," she gasped, reaching a new level of realization having finally said the words out loud. "Aunt Elizabeth is going to hit the roof! Poor Mama and Uncle Owen are going to be so disappointed in me. What if I lose my job?"

Continuing to hold LaRuth as they both had started to rock back and forth slightly, Billie shushed her distraught friend, "Just take a breath. You right. It's gon' be hard getting through telling everybody but no matter what, you got me and you got your family — even if they might be mad or disappointed. It's not the end of the world. And you ain't gon' lose your job. Trust me, everything is gon' be alright."

As LaRuth anticipated, Lucille was disappointed but also concerned for her daughter.

"It's gon' be alright, baby," Lucille sighed. "Lord a mercy! You ain't the first girl done found herself expectin' with no husband and you won't be the last. I know you is upset but you said Marvin say he gon' stay with you and marry you as soon as he can. For now, I want to believe him. But even if he don't, we still gon' be alright."

Given all that she had seen and experienced in life, Lucille knew that there were many much worse situations than the one they were facing.

As LaRuth also had anticipated, Elizabeth was fit to be tied.

"But I know I raised you better than that, LaRuth," she chided. "You know you can't trust no man a hundred percent — especially when you ain't got no wedding ring."

"Yes, ma'am," LaRuth offered, saying as little as possible and sitting as still as a statue. It didn't matter that she was a grown, 23-year-old, employed, college graduate. At that moment, she felt like her old fifth-grade self, trying to explain how she wound up in the principal's office. For a few moments, she'd almost wished to be back in fifth grade dealing with that problem rather than the current one.

"Well, we gon' figure this out. Maybe you gon' have to come back home but we gon' figure it out. I ain't happy 'bout all of this but you know you can always come home. We gon' make sure everything is alright."

Figure it out they did. LaRuth continued her job until Ground Hog Day in February 1965, when she gave birth, prematurely, to me at Forrest Memorial Hospital, the same hospital where Aunt Elizabeth worked as a nurse's assistant. After a brief maternity leave, LaRuth returned to her job at the Extension Service. However, given the distance from Augusta to Forrest City, everyone agreed that she would stay in Augusta during the week and come to Forrest City on the weekends. Baby Walter would stay with Elizabeth and Owen. Thus, like her mother, LaRuth became the second Eldridge woman to surrender a child to Elizabeth to raise, though Elizabeth needed help herself since she still had her job at the hospital. Consequently, Lucille's sister Dessie Mae, who lived in Forrest City as well, would keep me during the day when Elizabeth was at work.

Instead of being exhausted by the presence of a baby in the house, Elizabeth and Owen were invigorated. It certainly didn't hurt that my mother had given me Owen as my middle name. Both were quite pleased and doted on me as if I were their own — which in many respects I was, especially during the week when they had me to themselves. For them, everything revolved around taking care of the new baby. I'm told that Papa, as I came to call him, was very taken with having an infant in the house. He was so attentive and concerned for my well-being that one night he refused to go to bed when I suffered from a cough that wouldn't seem to subside. It turned out to be nothing serious, but he was not comfortable taking any chances and stayed up with me until he was sure I was okay.

Lucille was enamored with her grandson as well. That my first name was Walter made me even more cherished. She never entertained the idea of asking her daughter to name a child after her late husband but the fact that my mother had done so meant more to her than she could describe. Sometimes the poignancy of a little boy named Walter after she had dreamed of one of her own so many years ago was too much for her to take in.

A year and a half later, even though LaRuth and Marvin still had not married, they welcomed another baby, my sister, Jacqueline. However, with the birth of a second baby, everyone agreed that LaRuth needed to be closer to help. By this time, she had begun a teaching job in Augusta and was able to find a similar position in the nearby town of Palestine, only seven miles and fewer than 15 minutes from Forrest City.

Jackie's arrival added a new dynamic to the house. Even as small children, we loved each other dearly — except when we didn't. While we were each other's fiercest friends, we could also be the staunchest of adversaries. My efforts at being the "big" brother often occasioned our tiffs. Jackie was not nearly as talkative as I was and I often spoke and answered for her. Nevertheless, she had her own way of making her feelings known.

"Walter," Uncle Owen cautioned in mild reproach, "Stop bossing your sister around over that little guitar."

"It's a ukulele, Papa, and I'm not bossing her," I replied. "I'm just showing her how to use it right."

Moments later, I cried out in pain. Having had enough of my "showing," Jackie hit me over the head with the little guitar.

"I guess that wasn't the way you showed her, was it?" Papa chuckled.

Life for our multi-generational family unit fell into a comfortable enough routine and everyone assumed their respective roles. Aunt Elizabeth, or Momo as Jackie and I called her, ruled the roost as matriarch. Papa continued to serve as a refuge for my mother as he had always done and became a similar safe haven for my sister and me when Momo was on the warpath. LaRuth followed in the hierarchy as "second mother" after Momo.

"Boy!" exclaimed Papa in mock derision. "Didn't you see my foot?" after I ran over his toe riding my tricycle.

"Papa, didn't you see me riding?" I answered, oblivious to my insolence but evidently secure in the adoration of my grandfather.

Even as she laughed herself along with her husband and LaRuth, Elizabeth cautioned, "Owen, you gon' spoil that boy rotten."

Momo's love for her "grandchildren" did not cloud her sense of duty as the resident parent in charge. Discipline and order remained her love languages.

"What's wrong?" LaRuth asked, walking into the house after coming home from work and finding me wiping away tears.

"Nothing's wrong," Momo answered before I could reply to my mother and as I tried to silence my sniffles. "I just had to get a switch to those legs."

"What happened?" she queried, looking at me sympathetically for an answer.

"He was outside acting like he don't have no home training! I caught him and that little boy down the street — Clemmie — peeing outside by the hedges! When the bathroom is right here inside the door! Thank goodness they were in the backyard!" she pronounced, apparently still offended.

Suppressing a smile at the thought of me relieving myself outside of Aunt Elizabeth's house while also empathizing with my recent spanking, my mother gave me a pitying nod but pressed her lips together as the only other acknowledgment of her compassion for my predicament, determined not to ignite a squabble over the appropriateness of Momo's mode of correction. We both understood in our respective ways that that was life — hers and mine.

What had become a familiar rhythm for all of us was disrupted when my parents married in May of 1970 and our family unit of four moved to Pine Bluff. While she very much wanted the respectability of marriage for LaRuth, Elizabeth had not thought ahead enough to realize that LaRuth's marriage would result in a relocation. Our moving away was not part of her plan. In fact, she unsuccessfully tried to convince my parents that she should keep my sister and me while they went off to start their married life.

Mama Ceal was pleased that her faith in my father had been well-placed and that my parents had married. Given that he was nearly 20 years older than my mother though, she recognized that his patience with my sister and me as small children was intermittent. Still, she admired him for the resolute way he endeavored to take care of his family. While some might call him cheap, it didn't matter to him as he was determined not to spend money on frivolous things or on tasks that he could do himself — and there was plenty that he could do. In addition to taking care of his 1956 Chevrolet Bel Air, he kept up the household car, changing the oil, rotating the tires, and performing most routine maintenance. Appliance repairmen, carpenters, electricians, plumbers, and the like would have gone broke if they had to depend on Marvin Pryor for business. All of those jobs he handled for our family himself. And I, as his compliant assistant, had a front row seat, passing him tools as requested, holding the flashlight, taking required measurements, and trying to give the appearance of keeping up with his teachings while being often perplexed and mostly disinterested.

Like my grandmother, he was an avid gardener. From the time I was in fourth or fifth grade until I graduated from high school, my sister and I received numerous lessons on using a rotary tiller and a push plow to learn how to prepare the ground at the end of our house to plant and grow tomatoes, corn, green beans, cucumbers, peas, squash, potatoes, peppers, melons, and all kinds of greens.

"Nope," corrected my father. "Try it again. It's not straight."

This was his direction after my second attempt at pushing a plow down a row in recently tilled ground to hold whatever seeds we were planting that day.

"Keep your eye on the spot where I put the stick at the end of the row and keep the wheel pointed to it."

"Yes, sir," I answered, the only acceptable reply to a man of his generation who brooked no lip nor sighs of exasperation from children, regardless of their age. Any frustration I was feeling was swallowed and, hopefully, my third attempt would be my last — at least on that row.

It wasn't.

My grandmother also admired the fact that my father attended church and loved that he was a well-regarded singer. I admired him for that as well. The first time we went to church after moving to Pine Bluff and I saw my father in the choir stand at Barraque Street Missionary Baptist Church, I was surprised. Until that moment, I had no idea that he sang. I am not sure what I thought when he stood up for a solo, but I almost gasped in amazement to hear his rich baritone voice singing *"How Great Thou Art"* to numerous "Amens" and nods from an appreciative congregation.

If there needed to be yet another point of connection between Lucille and her son-in-law, he had it in spades: they both loved fishing. Me, not so much.

The first time my father took me fishing, it couldn't have been long after we had moved to Pine Bluff. Thankfully, he brought my sister as well. Our early morning excursion started with a trip to the bait shop. While our father was getting minnows, crickets, and worms for the fish, he gave Jackie and me almost free reign to pick out whatever snacks we wanted. Chips — Bugles to be exact — cookies, peanuts, and Ding Dongs, and a few kinds of candy were our selections to go along with the canned potted meat, Vienna sausages, crackers and cheese that he had already packed for our lunch. For the novice fishers, that first trip was all about the snacks and the "picnic in a boat" that we were having. We couldn't have cared less whether we caught any fish. Because we had each other, my sister and I avoided the boredom of the hours we spent on the lake when the novelty of the snacks wore off. Future trips without my sister cemented for me that rising before dawn to spend eight hours or more fishing was not my idea of the perfect way to enjoy a Saturday.

Putting aside the bills and advertising flyers that she had just retrieved from the mailbox one summer afternoon in 1970, LaRuth focused her attention on the envelope with the familiar handwriting and Forrest City return address. In addition to the letter that her mother had sent her, there was another shorter letter to five-year old Walter and soon to be four-year-old Jackie.

"You've got a letter," she called to us as we played in our bedroom at the back of the house in Pine Bluff that we had moved into following my parents' wedding, a small family gathering of less than 20 people at Momo's and Papa's house.

She shook her head in near disbelief for a few moments as she considered the rapid and unconventional way her life had unfolded since college. Seven short years ago, she could not have imagined all that would have happened. On this sweltering day in August, she ticked off those "unimaginables" on her mental list: she was married (check), with two children (check), had moved away from Forrest City to live with her new family in Pine Bluff (check), and had accepted a teaching job in the small town of Altheimer, about 15 miles away (check). She was a long way from the young woman who left AM&N with aspirations to teach.

Whatever it was that my sister and I were playing, it all disintegrated into oblivion the moment my mother called to us that we had a letter. I'm not sure how, but we knew instinctively that getting mail was a big deal. Jumping onto our parents' bed as our mother unfolded our letter, we fidgeted with excitement until she started to read to us.

> *Dear Jackie & Walter,*
>
> *How are you? I hope you are okay. Do you like your new house in Pine Bluff? I can't wate to come see it. I miss you. Is you being a good girl and boy? You is growing up so fast. Here is a four leef clover I found yesterday in the gardin. I only found one but will send you another when I get one. You be a good boy and girl. Moma C. love you both. Give your mother and father a kiss for me. Love Moma Ceal*

We were thrilled to have a letter from Mama Ceal and even more excited a year or so later when my mother helped us write our first letter back to her. We continued the tradition of writing to her, usually when our mother called us to sit down and do it, until the hustle and bustle of junior high school and extracurricular activities diverted our attention and offered an acceptable excuse for ceasing. Still, occasionally, we would surprise her with a letter, which repaid us in abundance with her gratitude.

Visits from Mama Ceal were huge events for my sister and me because we loved her so much. We adored her for many reasons — not the least of which was that we knew she adored us as well. She also enjoyed a good joke, liked to play cards, and loved watching wrestling. While we shared her complete faith in the authenticity of the bouts as children, once we got older and wiser, no amount of proof could convince her that the matches were fake. Her unwavering devotion both amused us and made us love her even more.

"Are you staying for a week, Mama Ceal?" Jackie asked our grandmother in the back seat on our ride home from the Greyhound bus station, Jackie on one side of her and me on the other. She almost always took the bus when she came to visit unless, on occasion, another relative offered to drive her. To this day, the smell of bus diesel fuel always ushers a wave of nostalgia in me as it is so associated with my grandmother.

"If you'll have me," she answered with a wink.

"Of course," Jackie answered. "You should stay the whole month!"

Before the days of summer activities and youth sports programs, in addition to getting to spend time in the summer visiting both Momo and Mama Ceal in Forrest City and Newcastle, we also got time with Mama Ceal when she took a "vacation" from working for the Hortons and came to visit us. We loved her visits as we knew that they invariably included fried pies, fresh baked bread, homemade ice cream, new entrées, and cake and pie recipes to which she would treat us and our extended family of relatives and friends in Pine Bluff. They too loved her visits as she was always so full of life and laughter and cheerfulness.

"Mama Ceal, can we help you make the fried pies?" I asked.

"You sure can," she smiled. "Are you sure Jackie wants to help, too?"

"I do!" Jackie replied almost before our grandmother could get the question out.

"Okay, then," Mama Ceal replied. "Jackie, you stir the cinnamon into the apples in the pot. Start with a teaspoon and we'll see if we want to add more after we take a taste."

"Yes, ma'am," Jackie eagerly complied. "Why do you use dried apples when you make fried pies?

"I don't know, baby. That's what the recipe called for and that's what I've always done. I suspect it's because it takes a lot more work to season fresh apples and get them to the consistency we need."

"What can *I* do?" I interjected, feeling left out.

"You gon' help me with the dough. We need a cup of flour, a cup of water, and the stick of butter I have softening in that bowl. You see those over there?"

"Yes, ma'am."

"Okay, use your hand to mix the butter and flour together and try to get them as smooth as you can. Then, I'll show you how to add the water."

There were so many moments like this that Lucille had missed with LaRuth as a child. However, what a blessing it was that she could now enjoy new ones with her grandchildren. No one could have told her how truly amazing it could be to soak up the love of grandchildren or how even bigger her heart could grow to love them in return.

She noticed how intently I was working on the dough. She could tell I was trying to get it exactly right and no amount of encouraging me to relax would make a difference.

Jackie sighed. "Can we play Kings Corner when the pies are done? Are you still gon' make homemade ice cream?"

"Well, let's finish the pies first and we'll see," laughed Lucille. "If you'll help me, we can make the ice cream tomorrow. Now, go find the cards, I imagine I can beat you in a game or two."

Lucille had studied my sister and me over the years. She thought I was a sweet boy but very serious, a product of Elizabeth's influence she surmised. She could tell already that Jackie was more of her own person and had a feisty streak — and she loved it. She also loved that we both were getting good grades in school and she liked to think that we were growing to be nice children. Smart was good but nice was better in her mind. She had no idea what our futures held but she wanted to believe that they were to be good ones. She could feel a desire rising in her to wish new wishes and pray new prayers even though she had vowed that she would not ask more of God. In that moment, she gave herself permission to make new entreaties. This time though, her prayers would not be for college graduates, but rather for her grandchildren to be nice, happy people.

TWENTY-EIGHT

No matter how old I got, I never lost the excitement and joy of spending time with Mama Ceal. This was no less true in the months leading up to my graduation from Georgetown Law in May of 1990. Only this time, it was Mama Ceal's anticipation that was unmistakable. In her letters to me, she went from a few casual references that she was beginning to save for her trip to Washington, DC to inquiries about the cost of hotel rooms to suggesting that we host a reception for some of my friends and their families. Her later letters couldn't contain her elation and eventually she flat out admitted how excited she was to be coming.

During this same time, the Horton family had witnessed several months of declining health in Della Horton, who at this point had been my grandmother's employer for more than half her life. Although formally, they remained employer and employee, the two had become more like companions. Understandably, my grandmother was worried about her. But true to her personality, Mama Ceal clung to every possible shred of hope that Ms. Della would rally and return to a stronger, more stable state of wellbeing. Having the Washington trip to look forward to was a welcome ray of brightness to balance the growing concern and gloom regarding Ms. Della's waning vigor.

It was especially gratifying for me to observe Mama Ceal's increasing awareness of how folks outside of our family looked at my completion of law school. While it was certainly a big deal to her, she had not appreciated that others might be equally excited. As word spread, she was inundated with congratulatory messages and well wishes from not only her friends and neighbors but also from friends of the Horton family as well. It pleased her to no end that Mr. Gene, Mrs. Della's son, was telling everyone who listened. For someone who you could rarely find bragging, she could not suppress her delight over the greetings from others who shared her joy that she had a grandson graduating from law school. It made me happy that I made her proud.

In one of her first letters to me during this period, Mama Ceal jokes that she has already saved 50 pennies to apply to the cost of her bus ticket after updating me that the Hortons' great grandson Baxter had told her that he needed me to be his school's lawyer so that I could help their local community prevent the closure of their school and the plan to bus students to schools in Forrest City. Even though I had not yet graduated from law school or passed a bar exam, Baxter and his mother were happy to provide me with my first case as a lawyer.

> Route 1 Box 315
> Forrest City Ark
>
> Dear Walter
> Well this leave me all. hope you is the same give my love to Juliette & Donna. Say tell you that Calwell School needs you face there lawer they say they cant get a lawer to take there case it fare the school they Weunt to close it And Bus all to Forrest City. Baxter say he be with you all the way. Well I have 50 pennies to go on my ticket to Washington Oniell Bam Bem and all send there love to you. Well I Am in a Hurry But Weunted you to here from you. Mrs Della is about the same.
> Lave I love you
> Moma C.

Route 1 Box 315
  Forrest City, Ark

> *Dear Walter*
> *Well, this leve me ok. Hope you is the same. Give my love to Juliette. Oh Donna say tell you that Calwell School Kneed you fore there lawer. They say they cant get a lawer to take there case. It fore the school. They wount to close it and bus all to Forrest City. Baxter say that he be with you all the way. Well I have 50 pennes to go on my ticket to Washington (smile). Bam Bam and all send there love to you. Well I am in a hurry but wounted you to here from me. Mrs. Della is about the same.*
> *love I love you*
> *Moma C.*

In her next letter, the possible school closure is still top of mind for the Horton family and, consequently, for her. She forwards a newspaper clipping with a picture of Baxter participating in a petition drive to prevent the proposed closure along with his request that I come help. Yet, she also comes back to the topic of graduation. The imminence of the trip prompts her to ask for hotel costs so that she can *"really"* start saving for the trip. True to form, she adds a joke, this one that maybe she can come barefoot if it's warm enough since she needs new shoes.

Route 1 Box 315
  Forrest City, Ark

> *Dear Walter*
> *Well this is my weekly letter. Also a clipen of Baxter. He say so you can see why he kneed you here to show these law what happen (smile). This leve me ok. Hope you all is the same. Give my love to Juliette. Well we is haven lot of rain. Oh yes write and tell me what the hotels rooms is so I can realy start to saven my pennies. Of corse I don't have any shoes but it may be warm enough that I can bare foot it.*
> *Well I got to get this in the mail. love Moma C.*

> Route 1 Box 31
> Forrest City Ark
> Dear Walter,
> Well this is my weekly letter also a clipen of Baxter he say so you could see why he tried you here to shaue these Saw what hoppen (Smile) this leue me ok, hope you all is the same give my love to Juliette
> Well here is haven lot to say Oh yes Write and let my know what the Hotels Rooms is so I can realy start to sauen my Pennies of corse I don't have my Shoes but it may be warm enough that I can Barefoot it.
> Well I got to get this in the mail
> love momac

Mama Ceal always enjoyed receiving calls so I tried to do so periodically since I was not the letter writer that she was. In the following missive, she expresses her elation at our having spoken and also that she had relayed my admiration to our cousin, Selma Stegall, whose singing I had complimented. In addition to sending her best to Juliette, she admits that she is excited about the trip to Washington. She also mentions the bus strike because she thought she would be taking the bus — her long-distance mode of travel if not riding in a car — even though the family was planning to travel by plane. She had not even contemplated the idea of flying. She also gives me an update about Baxter, David, and Sarah, the Hortons' great grandchildren.

Dear Walter
   Oh it were so good to talk to you and [to hear] that you were ok. This leve me ok. I went to church and told Selma what you said. He say be sure to come to the church. Bam Bam and Connie Mae all send there love. Oh yes, give Juliette Hi fore me. Oh I am getten excited about comen to Washington. I hope the bus strak will be over. Sarah is durn good in school. She were on oner rol [honor roll]. Also Baxter & David.
   Well you be a good boy and pray fore me. Love Moma C.

The arrival of Easter meant that May, and the trip to Washington was right around the corner. Her excitement was building, and she was no longer questioning whether she was coming. She also indicates that she'd like to include time for her to visit — briefly — the Hortons' son, Russell, who lived outside of Washington and to see the house that he built.

> Hi Walter
> Well its getten clost. I hope you is ok. This leve me ok. And is getten excited two. Give my love to Juliette. Tell her I am looken fore an Easter egg if I can beat the dogs findin one. Every one here is durn pretty good. We is haven some cold weather but not like you all snow. Mr. Russel say that you had snow the 7 of April. Oh will you be able to take us out to his house one day while we are up there. I don't wount to stay, just wount to see it so you be plain [planning] it pleas. love Moma C.

Though not nearly often enough, I tried to write Mama Ceal occasionally. The following letter illustrates how happy she was to get a letter from me. It is also evident that she is practically bursting at this point — "I am so proud of you" — as more and more people were beginning to learn that she had a grandson graduating from law school. She was thrilled to update me that one of Mrs. Della's friends had visited and wanted to know the name of my law school. I believe the envelope she mentions sharing with the woman is the envelope from the graduation announcement. Not to forget anyone, she also sends greetings to Juliette and to my friend Shahryar Hakimi whom she had met when he accompanied me on one of my trips to Arkansas.

> Route 1 Box 315
> Forrest City Ark
>
> Dear Walter
>
> Well it were a Big Suprise to get a sweet letter from you so glad you is durn all. Well I dont know if Enything will be come of it But one of Mrs Della Friend were out here to see Mrs Della she met you on the Birth day of Mrs Della She wecented the School that you is in So I gave her the Inulop That you sent me She Weent to Send it to her Grand Daughter oh yes Will you pleas make some time fure us to go see Mr and Mrs Horton Just fure a visit becaus I dont weent to miss Eny thing (small) I am So Proud of you also Mr. Eugene Cousin were out her he Say I here your Grand Son is fenishen Law school he say I am Proud I ave him

Dear Walter

Well it were a Big suprise to get a sweet letter from you. So glad you is durn ok. Well I dont know if anything will become of it but one of Mrs Della Friend were out here to see Mrs Della. She wounted the shool that you is in so I gave her the envlop that you sent me. She wount to send it to her Grand Daughter. Oh yes Will you pleas make some time fore us to go see Mr and Mrs Horton just fore a visit becaus I dont wount to miss anything (smile). I am so proud of you. Also one of Mr Eugene Cousin were out here. He say I here your grandson is finishen law school. He say I am proud fore him and I know you is and I am proud fore you tow.

Also give Juliette my love. Also and Shah. Tell all of them to say a little pray for me. I am glad you had a Happy Easter. You be good and rember me in your prayers.

love you Moma C.

There is full blown excitement now as Mama Ceal is proposing a small reception or "drop in" for Juliette and her family along with any of my friends that I wanted to invite. She even suggests a possible menu. And she does not forget to remind me that she wants to visit Mr. Russell while she is in town.

Route 1 Bx 315
Forrest City Ark.

Dear Walter
Oh it were so good to here from you and that you is ok. this leve me are. Well here is a question do you want some of your Friends over Sunday even a while if so I will make some Sausage Balls & olive ball Cookies and Jackie can make some dip and punch I will bring a white table clouth and if Juliette faulks will be there invite them if you want me to I havent said any thing to Elizabeth or Laluth But you can deside when we get there Oh Wyoma say Hi and she is so happy for you she say she wish I could go but she is werken and half becaus they have a trailor and they have moved you be a good Boy love to Juliette love momma C.

Oh will you talk to mom Reussel ask if they will be home Friday even and will you plain to take us out there pleas

Route 1 Box 315
  Forrest City, Ark

   Dear Walter
   Oh it were so good to here from you and that you is ok. This leve me ok. Well here is a question. Do you wount some of your friends over Sunday even a while. If so, I will make some sausage balls & olive ball, cookies and Jackie can make some dip and punch. I will bring a white tablecloth and if Juliette folks will be there envite them if you wount me to. I haven't said anything to Elizabeth or LaRuth but you can decide when we get there. Oh Wyoma [Wyoming] say hi and she is so happy fore you. She say she wish I [could go but she is worken and [illegible] because they have a tralor and they moved. You be a good boy. Love to Juliette.
   love Moma C.
   Oh will you talk to Mr. Russel. Ask if they will be home Friday even [evening] and will you plain to take us out there pleas.

The time for my graduation is almost upon us and Mama Ceal is remembering to be prayerful that all goes as planned. She continues to get congratulatory calls from her friends and neighbors and is amused (and likely thrilled) that Mr. Gene is telling everyone he sees.

> Dear Walter
> Well it nat to vmuch longer be fore we will get to see you if its the Lord Will I pray every thing will go ok. Well dont wait vmy grand babie to heard [oncell] but get things to gather if you wecent that drop by on Sunday evening I have got lat of call fore good Wishis fore you Mr Eugene tell every one he talk to about you and Jackie also LaRuth some [Ymave] LaRuth but they all know me
>   love moma C.
> Say Hi to Juliette & Jackie

> *Dear Walter*
> *Well it is not much longer be fore we will get to see you if its the Lord will. I pray every thing will go ok. Well don't work my gandbabie to heard (Smile) but get things together if you wount that drop in on Sunday evening. I have got a lot of call fore good wishes fore you. Mr. Eugene tell every one he talk to about you and Jackie. Also LaRuth. Some know LaRuth but they all know me.*
> *love Moma C.*
> *Say hi to Juliette & Jackie*

In some respects, graduation weekend was a blur for me. While I tried to be mindful of hosting my family and ensuring they were having a good time, I was also caught up in the euphoria of finally finishing three long years of study and occasional hardship while juggling the many parties and gatherings my classmates and friends were having. Still, I recall several impromptu hugs and winks with my grandmother as well as brief interludes where I observed her reveling in the moment and seemingly floating on clouds.

Unfortunately, there was sad news from Newcastle that dampened the mood. Shortly after Mama Ceal had arrived in Washington, Mrs. Della died. This was a huge blow to my grandmother and presented a heartrending conflict. She was faced with the choice of staying for my graduation or leaving to return for the family funeral. It was especially anguishing for her as she wanted to do both. Ultimately, she chose to remain in Washington. While she missed the family funeral, fortunately, she was back home for the memorial service that was held later in the summer.

However, we did host a small open house reception at my apartment as Mama Ceal had hoped. In addition to our own family, my future wife (and then undisclosed fiancé) Juliette and her family were there, as were some of our friends from law school with some memers of their family. Mama Ceal was elated and kept a smile on her face practically the entire time.

I can only imagine how overjoyed her soul must have felt at the idea that her dream of sending my mother to college had led to two grandchildren who had graduated from both college and graduate school as my sister had also completed a master's program by the time of my law school graduation. (Unfortunately, Mama Ceal would not live to see my sister receive her doctorate degree.) I believe her heart was full.

The following year, Juliette and I were married and Mama Ceal's excitement about coming to the wedding seemed even greater than her excitement for my graduation. She loved Juliette and the two shared a mischievous spirit that kept them whispering and giggling with each other whenever we were together.

That she also was able to meet the first of her two great-grandchildren, my daughter Adjua, is bittersweet only in that she was not able to meet her second, my son Wade Osei. One of the last pieces of correspondence we have from her is a letter she sent to Adjua for her birthday along with a quick note to the rest of us.

When Mama Ceal died in 1995 after a bout with cancer, I spoke at the funeral and commented that being in her presence had always conjured for me the warmth and security of family. Now, whenever I recall my memories with her, I occasionally experience a tinge of sadness as I still miss her terribly and wish that she had lived to see more of how our lives unfolded. However, reminiscing about her evokes that same warm, secure feeling and a sense of gratitude for what she sparked in our family. I wonder how our lives might have been different had she not dreamt of my mother graduating from college and then been willing to make the sacrifice of sending her away in order to make that dream possible. Would my mother have gone to college? Would I have been born at all or attended law school? Would Mama Ceal's great-granddaughter have graduated from Wesleyan and gone to law school as well? Would her great-grandson have graduated from Harvard and graduate school in Italy? Where does the ripple end?

I can't say that I think of Mama Ceal every day. However, I do think of her often and how her influence continues to be felt in ways large and small. Her quilts still remind us of her kindheartedness. Our holiday tradition of making her chocolate coconut ball candy continues to rouse her love of Christmastime. And anytime I get a handwritten note or letter, it takes me back to some of my earliest memories: of letters I was not able to read, but that told me that I was important enough to receive mail. That I mattered.

This leaves me more than okay.

EPILOGUE

The day that I had set aside to visit the Horton family started out as a cloud-covered and dreary one. The forecast threatened rain. I couldn't escape the feeling that the anticipated weather might be an omen of things to come. I'm not sure why I was so concerned as the days leading up to the trip had gone particularly well. The first good sign was a prompt and positive response from the great granddaughter of Lee and Della Horton — Jennie Horton — who I contacted through social media to ask how to get in touch with her father. Her dad is John Horton, one of the children my grandmother had helped raise. Jennie replied with the phone numbers for both her parents and expressed her regret that she didn't live closer to be able to see me during my planned trip. She also mentioned how much she loved my grandmother.

Her kindness touched me, and I imagined Mama Ceal smiling.

The next positive sign was that when I shared my plans with my mother and asked her if she would travel with me, she immediately agreed — even expressing a small degree of enthusiasm, which is a big deal for her given her generally subdued demeanor.

Additionally, my ensuing text exchanges with John and his wife Donna yielded their excitement about our coming, an invitation to have lunch at their house, and an offer to go through "lots" of pictures, which caught me off guard as I wasn't expecting them to have pictures, but quickly assumed they were ones I had seen before. I also asked if Carl, John's brother, might be able to join us since I welcomed the chance to visit with him also. They assured me they would try to make that happen.

Weather aside, the lead-up to my trip should have quelled any reservations. Still, I was anxious.

As my mother and I made the drive, we chatted about a variety of topics. What was the latest news with Adjua and Osei? We agreed that the improvements to the county roads we traveled were long overdue. We laughed at remembered humorous moments with Mama Ceal and Momo. We speculated as to the possible plantings that we couldn't recognize in the fields we passed as likely rice or soybeans. Somewhere along the way, it dawned on me that it had been over 30 years since I had been to the place that Mama Ceal had called home for the majority of her life.

Taking the Wynne exit off Interstate 40, I was struck at how developed the area was, nothing at all like what I had last known. While I could remember trips to Newcastle as a child, taking gravel roads for part of the time, this journey was on paved roads the entire way. I had also remembered how desolate the road seemed; it had felt like there was absolutely nothing to see but long expanses of trees, fields, and undeveloped land. Now, the nothingness was populated with homes of varying sizes and stations. The houses weren't necessarily close to each other, some several hundred yards or more from their nearest neighbor but, compared to how unpopulated the stretch of road used to be, the difference was significant. I couldn't help but notice how suburban it felt and chuckled with my mother that the small town of Forrest City had become big enough to have a suburb. Large plastic garbage containers, apparently having been emptied earlier that day, sat at the road awaiting return to their places at their respective houses. In addition to the homes, a few churches, a fire station, and other business buildings dotted the landscape. The trip that, as a kid, had felt like such a long trek to get to Mama Ceal, passed very quickly — perhaps because there was so much more to look at and perhaps because time moved much slower for me as a child. However, as we neared our destination, all of these challenges to my recollection began to make me question whether I would feel closer to my grandmother or more distanced from her, given how so much of what I thought I remembered had changed.

But for the navigation system, I could have easily passed the right turn onto a road that I had gone down innumerable times before. Nothing looked familiar. Houses here and there on large plots of land could have been anywhere in rural Arkansas until I crested a small hill. The frame of an old hollowed-out gin in the distance on my right and the unmistakable outline of a small store further ahead on the left reassured me that I had not forgotten everything. Another right turn onto a gravel drive led us to John and Donna's home. I wondered if the truck in the driveway whose bottom was covered in mud belonged to Carl.

Getting out of the car, we were glad that the drizzle had stopped and the mild temperature had held. John greeted us at the door and welcomed us inside. Carl was there as well — the owner of the truck I had noticed. We all gave each other hesitant but genuine hugs and moved into the kitchen for lunch at Donna's urging. She explained that there really weren't places around that were conducive to visiting so they felt lunch at home made more sense.

After we sat at their kitchen table and John offered a prayer, we engaged in small talk, catching up regarding each other's families, discussing how much change we had observed on the drive, and noting articles from Donna's estate and antique business that decorated the kitchen. We enjoyed a delicious lunch of meatloaf (which I ate — even though I don't eat red meat — since it felt rude not to do so after Donna had gone to such trouble *and* I felt like Mama Ceal would have wanted me to), potato casserole, green beans, corn, rolls, and, of course, iced tea. Trying not to rush the meal but anxious to get my "tour" started, I mentioned my desire to go look at the store and houses.

Although we could have walked the few hundred yards across the road, Carl offered to drive me after my mother, John and Donna all elected not to join us. He forewarned me that Mama Ceal's room along with the shed to which it was attached had burned some years ago. Their father had accidentally caused a fire by plugging in a heater that set some straw ablaze. I was deflated as I had sentimentalized a moment of being overcome standing in Mama Ceal's room, returning to the space that had meant so much to her and that held so many memories of our time together. I had wanted to confirm my rememberances even though I knew her things had long since been removed. I had wanted to reconcile the pictures in my head. I had wanted to stand where she stood — one last time. But it was not to be. Swallowing my disappointment, internally I wished that someone had thought to mention that her room no longer existed before we had arrived.

Because the store sat at the beginning of the drive to the houses, we stopped there first. Entering the building prompted a memory of Mr. Lee offering Jackie and me candy as children. I must have been no more than age four or five since he died in 1970. Carl confirmed my belief that there had been a candy counter near the cash register and also the location of a freezer case that held ice cream and popsicles. The exposed wood planks that comprised the walls of the store had been painted although something about them felt like they weren't much disturbed in the forty plus years since I had last seen them. Framed patriotic sayings, newspaper clippings, photographs of local scouting troops and other memorabilia hung on the walls. These mementos were relatively current but the aura of the store conjured an earlier time of people like my grandfather signing on accounts or washerwomen untying coins from knotted handkerchiefs to pay for the provisions they had purchased.

Carl gave me a tour of the entire building, much of it I realized I had never seen before since my time in the store was usually focused on the candy counter. I could tell Carl was proud to show me the craftsmanship in the structure his forebearers had built. We then moved over to the area that I had been most interested in seeing.

Less than 30 minutes earlier, I was convinced it would have been better if I had known before I arrived that my grandmother's room was gone. Perhaps I thought that my managed expectations might have diminished my disappointment. In retrospect, no amount of advance warning could have made me feel any less cheated.

I looked intently for an outline of the building, some trace of the foundation or indentations in the ground, any remnants to suggest that a structure used to be there. I wanted something more than just my memory or images captured in pictures to testify to what had been. Where was the artifact that verified that the room where I helped her heat up water for our bath — and where we watched wrestling — had stood here? Could I identify some sign that this was the place where she had finished numerous quilts and needle point creations and crocheted throws? Was anything left after the fire to document this as the site of the place where our family matriarch had spent so much of her time holding her heart, dreaming naïve dreams, praying for our family, willing herself to be content?

My efforts were in vain. Instead, the place where Lucille had lived for so many years looked like a regular, unimportant patch of ground. My sorrow rose anew. There were no tears, but my melancholy felt bottomless. Seeing that there was no relic to point to, not even an empty crevice or void to prove that something had been there, underscored my sense of loss. With my grandmother gone, I had needed there to be something tangible, some evidence, some archaeological find beyond memories and photographs to substantiate that she had been there, in that spot.

Pulling it together, I reacquainted myself with the orientation of where Mama Ceal's room had been in relation to Mrs. Della's house, and John and Carl's childhood home. Despite the fact that I had been there tons of times as an adult, the most prominent recollections were still those from my childhood. Only on this day, everything was smaller, closer, and less imposing than my remembrances. I asked Carl a few questions about other areas of the property and tried to edit the current scene to reconcile it with the one in my mind. After Carl showed me a small but comfortable cabin he had built, we returned to join the others.

Looking through the photo albums that Donna had meticulously kept with categorized and labeled sections and descriptions, I was floored at the number of pictures of my grandmother — and also of my mother — that I had never seen before. Once over the initial shock, my next reaction was anger which I was careful to conceal. All I could think was "why do you have these pictures of my grandmother?" as I forced myself to keep smiling. It soon dawned on me that these were not pictures that I had a right to expect to have seen or that had belonged to my family. No one had taken them from us. These were *their* family's pictures in *their* family albums. It was then that I realized that as much as Mama Ceal was my family, she was also a part of theirs as well. We knew that my grandmother had felt that the Hortons were like family to her, but I had not fully gotten that they — or at least some of them — felt similarly. As difficult as it may be for some to believe, they really did love her in the best ways they knew how. While I had not reflexively assumed that they only considered her as "the help," I had not conceived of their relationship as being as intimate, as heartfelt as it apparently was.

Even as I reevaluated my lack of appreciation for the depth of the employer-employee-extended family connection they shared, I still had lingering doubts that had taken on a whole new level of complexity, given this latest information. The speed of my mind fueled numerous questions in rapid succession: had Lee and Della Horton really treated Mama Ceal with a level of respect that was appreciably different or better than other White people of that time? Did they pay her a fair wage? Were some family using her nickname as a means of keeping her in her place as opposed to as a term of affection? Why didn't anyone ever think of providing her with access to hot water in her room? What insight might have been revealed if the responses to those questions ran counter to the benevolent narrative we had come to believe? The answers would remain elusive.

As we continued to look through the pictures, a number of them evoked questions which John and Carl willingly answered. I learned about a trip to Shreveport, Louisiana that Mama Ceal had taken with them to visit their maternal grandparents. My mother subsequently supplemented their stories with an anecdote about how Mama Ceal stayed at the home of the maid who worked for John and Carl's grandparents and that the two women who had formed a friendship during that visit had reunited decades later after Mama Ceal had gone to live with my mother.

As Carl and John recalled memories of my grandmother, I noted, again with some degree of surprise, the genuine emotion in their recollection of their time growing up with her. They remembered licking the mixing bowls when she baked. They recalled their prank of sneaking up behind her to untie her apron strings while she was working in the kitchen. They remembered how great her pancakes were and driving her in a trailer behind the tractor to see her old house that she shared with the grandfather I never knew. They remembered using that same tractor and trailer to take her fishing. And her making popcorn for herself, them and Mrs. Della as they watched wrestling on Saturday afternoons.

I was coming to understand what my grandmother had known but that we had perhaps questioned: they loved her, too. Of course, she should be included in their family photo albums. In many ways, she was a part of their family and belonged to them, too. While this speaks of the people the Hortons were (and are), it also speaks of the person that she was, which I find even more remarkable given the time and circumstances she navigated.

For years, I could not fully understand how a person who had survived such trauma as a child and such obstacles as an adult could become the grandmother who I knew. Her ever cheerful, loving demeanor would tempt you to believe that hers had been a storybook existence. I was also intrigued by the idea of a Black woman with an eighth-grade education, living in the rural South taking up the practice of writing letters. Both topics led me in directions I had not anticipated or necessarily been prepared to go.

Exploring my grandmother's and mother's communication challenges forced me to acknowledge and explore mine. Their story required me to make adjustments to my own — for which my immediate family is grateful. Pointing out the dysfunction they experienced was a touchstone for revealing the impacts of family dynamics I had packed away out of self-protection and also simple avoidance. All fodder for sessions with my therapist.

Equally impactful and more distressing was examining the racial climate of my grandmother's time, which I had initially classified as a dark, faraway time before there was some measure of racial progress. The Summer of 2020 and the social unrest that captured the world's attention, underscored how threatened, insecure, and deceptive that the extent of societal growth was. The more parallels between her life and mine in relation to our respective racial climates, the more frustrated I became. I was particularly demoralized that Mama Ceal's great grandchildren must grapple with many of the same types of challenges related to race and equity that she had to face. Why must my daughter and her partner, Breanna, be mindful of areas of the country that might be hostile to same-sex couples when planning a drive cross country? Why does my son feel safer and less stressed living in Italy than walking around a town in Florida? As Marvin Gaye sang, it's enough to make me "wanna holler and throw up both my hands."

But there stands before me my grandmother's story. In the face of seemingly insurmountable obstacles, how did she build a family that within one generation sent a child to college, within two generations sent one to law school, and within three generations one to Harvard? How did she come to be such a prolific letter writer who realized that she could share her love through her thoughtfulness if not a wealth of material resources? How did she have the wherewithal to take charge of circumstances that left her without a husband and frequently without her child and still create an existence that would have otherwise seemed improbable at best? How did this person who was devalued in the larger society figure out how to master the impractical and find a way not only to be content with her life but hopeful for her future?

Maybe it was her willingness to be brave enough, vulnerable enough, foolish enough to exercise a degree of faith and hope that the next day could be better than the previous one in spite of the surrounding circumstances suggesting it wouldn't. She beat the odds stacked against her as a little girl, ultimately rising above her early years of family neglect and dysfunction to create a family rich in tradition and mutual affection. Although she didn't have a model for how she might send her child to college when she first conceived of the idea, she put the wheels in motion that led to that exact result. She learned to value the brief time with her husband without becoming noticeably bitter at his loss so early in their marriage. Armed only with her eighth-grade education, she took up the practice of writing letters, perhaps as a means of bringing calm but also as a way to keep her family connected. Without any signs or indications that she would be successful in her efforts, Mama Ceal did what she could to make her small world better, and in doing so impacted a much larger one. She prayed and hoped and believed for the better that was to come. Through the power of her life and her faith — and her love, most of all, it did come.

ACKNOWLEDGEMENTS

That you are holding this book in your hands, reading it on your e-reader or listening to it means that I am somewhere feeling exceptionally grateful. The idea for this book was not mine but my wife's. Juliette was aware of the cache of letters that I had accumulated during my time in law school and following our marriage. When we then learned more details of my grandmother's early life, she immediately said to me "You should write a book." And I immediately dismissed the idea. Because of the respect and love I have always held for good writing, I decided that I did not measure up to that standard and that attempting such an undertaking was foolish.

And yet, at the start of Covid, anticipating a lot of time on my hands as a corporate role was about to end, I ignored my lack of confidence and decided to take a stab at writing this book. In less than five pages, I captured the story of what I knew about my grandmother's life and thought to myself "Now what? How do I turn this into a book?" Deciding to contact a friend of my sister-in-law, Joelle, I texted Tatsha Robertson, writer, editor, co-author of The Formula, and Editor-in-Chief of The Root. I explained to her that I wanted to write a book but had no clue what I was doing or how to even start. I confessed that my first attempt at writing had yielded only a few pages and I didn't know what to do to make progress. How fortunate I am that Joelle and Tatsha are friends and that she responded to my message. She introduced me to Jeff Ourvan and his writing workshops aptly titled The Write Workshop. I was able to join one of his workshops which he was holding by Zoom because of the pandemic. After numerous submissions and critique sessions, and over the course of three years, I completed the manuscript that is the foundation for this book.

There are so many people I want to thank as it indeed took "a village."

Thank you, God, for my life and the wealth of family and of love that I have enjoyed.

It is wonderful when you can get lost in a book and even more so when you can find yourself in one. I am grateful for and acknowledge the inspiration, motivation, encouragement, inclusion, examples, poignancy, validation, and joy in the works of Isabel Wilkerson, James Baldwin, Ta-Nehisi Coates, Tiya Miles, Walter Mosley, Octavia Butler, James McBride, Yaa Gyasi, and Robert Jones, Jr., among so many others. You are the reason I was intimidated to start this journey.

As is evident, I hold a profound love and gratitude for my family. I am thankful for my late father and for my mother, who held before me a quiet but clear expectation that I was to do well in school, which strengthened my love of reading and encouraged my desire for scholastic achievement. Even as I questioned my ability to write a book, the fact that I had done well in school spurred a confidence in me that overcame my competing self doubt and hesitance to take the first step. That gratitude includes of course Mama Ceal, Momo and Papa, Aunt Dessie, Selmer & Bam Bam, and the Eldridge, Hatch and Pryor branches of my family as theirs was the grounding which made me who I am. Thank you also to my extended family of Barraque Street Missionary Baptist Church and specifically to the set of families who, though not related by blood (except for one), that became a family created by choice and that gave me numerous "aunts, uncles and cousins" — the Pryor, Floyd, Jackson, Jones, and Callaway families. In regard to foundational networks of support, I am similarly thankful to those who poured into me over decades and whose influences I don't take lightly: the faculty and staff of Altheimer School, Dollarway Schools, and Hendrix College. I have also enjoyed overwhelming support from friends who became family and who held me accountable by inquiring how the book was coming, asking me to read excerpts for them, and reminding me how invested they were in my telling this story as it stood in proxy for so many of their own family stories. You know who you are — Shepherd Park Crew, MV Six, and our Chicago crew of friends.

I have to make a special call out to my mother and to my sister, Jacqueline Pryor, who did so much of the grunt work in helping me find pictures and follow up on vague recollections of stories that were not only insightful but critical to the scenes I was able to recreate. Thanks to my cousin Dianne Hatch who was a source for family history and to my mother's girlfriends Carrol Tillman,

Billie Pryor, and Grace Charles for sharing their recollections and anecdotes.

Thank you to Jeff Ourvan, my mentor, agent and friend who guided me through this process even when we had no idea where it was going or whether it would end in anything we would want to publish. My heartfelt thank you to my fellow "workshoppers" who welcomed me immediately and who buttressed my confidence through their support. The initial group of Aliah Wright, Haji Shearer, Jaye Landon, and Jeremy Goldstein were my first set of compatriots and to whom I am so indebted. Having them see me as a writer was everything. The group contracted at various points but also grew to include Danielle Arceneaux, Jocelyn Bystrom, Bianca Ambrosio, Amina Ali, Sam Israel, and Jennifer Gil-Velazquez. All of these incredibly talented people in the workshops shared insights and comments that played key roles in how my writing evolved and some also served as readers when I finished the manuscript. Please look for their books as I am sure you will find them as enjoyable as I did.

To those who served as readers/reviewers, your critiques, questions, comments and excitement have meant so much to me. Thank you, Dr. Alice Hines, Juanita Sealy-Williams, Saul Williams, Tatsha Robertson, Stacey Abrams, Dr. Daniel Black, Doug Blackmon, Eric Holder, Becky Pittman, Rev. Courtenay Miller, Rodney Lockett, and Rev. Otis Moss III.

I am also grateful to the Horton family for sharing their time, hospitality, memories, and photographs; to Naomi Rosenblatt of Heliotrope Books, who loved and embraced this story from the moment she learned about it,; and to Jen Maguire, who has been a wonderful partner in promoting it. Thank you.

Finally, thank you, dear reader, for your interest in this book. I hope you have found it time well spent. I also hope that you might be inspired to investigate the sheroes and heroes of your own family — deceased and living. Call their names. Celebrate them. Tell your children and loved ones about them. And whisper a quiet prayer of gratitude that they lived.

Write for your dead. Tell them a story. What are you doing with this life? Let them hold you accountable." — Alexander Chee

photo ©Jackie Hicks

AUTHOR

Walter Pryor is a son of the South, the Black Church, and a strong family unit of resilient, formidable women. He is a cum laude graduate of Hendrix College, the only Black student in the college's history to have been awarded the President's Medal, and a graduate of Georgetown University Law Center. His professional career has spanned a myriad of sectors in the legal arena, in both large and small law firms, the U.S. Department of Justice, Capitol Hill, corporations, and higher education. He is passionate about education and has devoted a significant amount of time to serve on boards and volunteer work in that space. *This Leaves Me Okay* is his first book.

www.ingramcontent.com/pod-product-compliance
Lightning Source LLC
Chambersburg PA
CBHW031317160426
43196CB00007B/576